MW00874526

The Prophecy of Genesis One

By Francis Gregory Febus

New Jerusalem Publishing

Table of Contents

3

5

The Dedication of the Temple

- On that day there shall be no more seasons

- The moed ceases and comes into its REST.

The Foundation of the World

- The Blood of Abel

All Things

- A Universal World View

- God so loved the world

- He Saved the Body

- All Things

- Things in Subjection

- Creatures and All Things

- Things are Given Life

- The Creation of all Things

Editor: Patrick Fullam

Book cover design: Michael Blume

To Helen

Preface

At last, we have completed this volume after several events, which diverted our attention to the care of our ailing mothers. This work is the result of approximately six years of study, although we feel that the project will continue through subsequent articles and sundry material. Genesis One viewed as a prophetic document sets the stage for a revolutionary view for the Church at large. Unfortunately, the present positions taken on the study of Genesis One disallow any notions of engaging upon its intended relationship to the prophetic record. After an era of discovery and research, the natural man has succeeded in undermining several basic assumptions the Church has held for centuries. We have become vulnerable through our unwillingness to thoroughly assess holy writ as originally delivered to the ancient world devoid of the influences of Western philosophy. At times, much of the documentation in this book will appear to be a continuation of an old concern ardently disputed throughout Church history. It will also seem as though its author is postulating something new. As one wades through its pages, one will experience the feeling of liberation as myths disrobed before our eyes. The clarity and simplicity of the Gospel a reconciled to its organic origins by dissociating itself from the fog of dispensationalism.

Our adventure begins with *"A word on interpretation."* We do not endeavor to introduce methods of interpretation that are foreign to the distillation of scripture, but they may seem strange to those who have studied modern Western methods of analysis. Conversely, we have chosen scholars of the nineteenth century who were not bound to the biblical correctness of our era to assist us in our enterprise. Our methods concur with the methods utilized by many an astute scholar of Biblical exegesis. Milton Spencer Terry, James Glasgow, and F.W. Farrar, each of whom has written extensively on the subject of interpretation were influential in the assembly of this book. In general, we have come to the same conclusions as to the scholars mentioned above but differ in other areas of concern. We do not mirror all of their conclusions, but we do employ their methods of interpretation.

For example, we tend to eschew the philosophic views and methods generated from the ancient Greeks, whose views are widespread and even fundamental to the study of modern exegesis. These methods have become a major stumbling block in the pursuit of Biblical interpretation, and its influences are in every lexicon, library, and seminary. The task of getting to the bottom of things is, therefore, daunting. When analyzing a text, we endeavor to "see what's truly there" as opposed to yielding to the worn narratives recommended to us by well-meaning instructors. Thus, the exploration of the seven day week is not treated as an event in cosmological history but interpreted as it was originally intended... like an ancient prophetic style of poetry easily recognized by those addressed (audience relevance).

We venture into the overlooked Hebraic values of such expressions as "Heaven and Earth," "Sun, Moon and Stars," "Created," "Day and Night," "Light and Darkness," "Dust of the Earth," and "Living Soul."

Other subjects related to the misapprehension of modern scholarship include an entire chapter devoted to the universalization of major portions of holy writ as they perpetuate the cosmological narrative imposed upon the

Hebrew text of Genesis One. This influence is indeed staggering with the invasion of its wayward views upon the unsuspecting mass of Christian believers.

There is a chapter dedicated to The Feasts of the Lord as we discuss them briefly about their prophetic underpinning with the seven days of Genesis One. The Feasts are an integral part of prophecy, and its acknowledgment is vital if we are to view their function regarding Genesis One. We conclude our study with a portion entitled, *"The Breath of God,"* which ties the imagery of 1 Thessalonians 4:17 with the imagery of Genesis 2:7 as God gathers His people through the breath, reputation and identity of God's Shem, or Name.

Introduction

The seven day week recorded in Genesis One possesses far greater consequences prophetically than many are aware. It is beyond doubt the bedrock upon which all prophetic forms commence. That is quite a mouthful given the fact that the first chapter of Genesis is generally assumed by many to be an accounting of cosmic historical events that transpired approximately six thousand years ago! The contemporary view of Genesis One as mere cosmology has succeeded in conditioning generations of Bible students to a skewed view of scripture. We say this because the modern view of Creation is as an event or a series of events consigned to the ancient past of human existence. However, in actuality, the purposes of Genesis One was to prophetically structure and channel the absolute intent of holy writ from the shadow of its beginning to the illumination of its fulfillment. This principle is succinctly stated in the following passage of scripture, although the majority of Bible students today would not realize the application of its principle to the first chapter of Genesis.

Isaiah 46:9-10

9 Remember the former things of old: for I am God, and there is none else; I am God, and there is none like me,
10 **Declaring the end from the beginning** and from ancient times the things that are not yet done, saying,
My counsel shall stand, and I will do all my pleasure: KJV

Isaiah 41:4

4 Who hath wrought and done *it*, calling the generations from the beginning? I the Lord, the first, and with the last; I *am* he. KJV (See also Isaiah 48:3)

The following quotation expresses the prophetic "bookend" strategy of the Genesis – Revelation paradigm employed by the LORD in his word. Genesis is aptly referred to by author Milton Terry as, "The Apocalypse of Creation" for its creation/ de-creation motif. The symbiotic function of these two volumes (Genesis and Revelation) should be reconsidered to understand their overall import in holy writ.

"We prefer, accordingly, to call this first section of the Hebrew Scriptures an Apocalypse of creation. It is as truly a sevenfold revelation of a beginning as the Apocalypse of John is a mystic revelation of an end. Both of these writings inculcate in emphatic form that the Lord God of Israel is the first and the last, the beginning and the end. The seven days of the cosmogony are no more to be interpreted literally than are the seven trumpets of the Apocalypse. Indeed, the repetitions of "God said" in Genesis suggest some analogies to be found in the sounding of the seven trumpets. At the sounding of the first trumpet the earth was smitten; at the second the sea; at the third the rivers and fountains; at the forth the sun; at the fifth the abyss; at the sixth the armies of the Euphrates were set loose; at the seventh, "great noises in heaven" announced the advent of the reign of the Lord and his Anointed... The days of Genesis are as symbolical as the

trumpets of the Apocalypse, and can no more be successfully identified (or shown to correspond) with ascertained aeons of geology and cosmical evolution than can the trumpets with successive historical events…The narrative is no more a treatise on natural science than it is an almanac. It is rather a pictorial object lesson, as profitable for the present age as for any period in the past."

Biblical Apocalyptics 1898 M.Terry p.44

Inherent Contradictions and Assumptions Of the Cosmic View of Genesis One

Once an assumption becomes the north star of our world view, it becomes nigh impossible to regard the apparent fallacies that are created by those same assumptions. A kind of cognitive dissonance envelops its supporters resulting in an abandonment of dissenting views; any meaningful examination of those views is never even attempted. Some of the notable inconsistencies regarding the modern cosmological view of Genesis One recorded on the following page. It is more than probable that some of these concerns have already entered the consciousness of our readers but disregarded them due to an adherence to a particular dogma, creed, or organizational allegiance.

- Vs.1 and Vs.2 imply that the heavens and the earth existed before day one of creation

- Vs. 1 and Vs.2 present contrasting statements between the creation of heaven and earth in Vs.1 and its apparent decay and chaos depicted in Vs.2

16

- Vs.3 light is created on day one without the aid of the Sun and was "created" again in Vs. 14 on day four

- Vs. 9, the waters are gathered together into one place. Therefore the land would be one unbroken mass. Where do we find geological evidence to support that assumption if that occurred only 6,000 years ago?

- Vs.20 the fowls were brought forth _by the waters_

- Vs. 24 _the earth_ brought forth cattle and creeping things and beasts of the field (not out of nothing as Westerners view of "create" infers).
- Man and beast are "created" out of dust.

- Vs.26 "Let us make man in our image and likeness…." Who is the "us" in that verse?

- Chapter 2 Vs.1 "Thus the heavens and the earth were finished and _all the hosts of them_." If this is a summation of Chapter One, where are the "hosts" in Chapter One?

- Chapter 2 Vs. 4 "These were the generations (birthings) of the heavens and the earth when they were created IN THE DAY when the Lord God created the heavens and the earth." Where are these "generations" (birthings) represented in Genesis One? Did the Lord create the heavens and the earth in one day inferred in chapter two vs. four?

- Six days are assumed to be six 24hour intervals of time, but the seventh day is missing the designation, "evening and the morning" as the days that preceded it.

- Chapter two discusses the events of creation in detail but not in the order as presented in Chapter One. Does this indicate a "second creation," as some have proposed? Does this indicate a huge mishap in the recording of the sacred text, or are we misreading it all together?

The remedy for this confusion:

- Consider approaching the narrative of Genesis One through its prophetic value as opposed to a series of cosmological events of the distant past.

- Pursue the prophetic language and themes initiated within Genesis One and continue to reemphasize its patterns consistently throughout the Bible.

- Recognize and implement the Eastern Hebraic tradition of its written expression, style, and structure in our interpretation of Holy Writ.

- Comprehend the importance of the Feasts of Israel and the 70 Weeks of Daniel as the foundational patterns by which all redemptive prophecy finds its form. This motif is founded directly and indirectly upon the seven-day pattern initiated in Genesis One.

To identify the objectives of Genesis One, we must acknowledge its aims. Was the purpose of Genesis One to chronicle the dawn of man and the creation of the universe …or should it be consigned to a mere folktale for religious consumption? Unfortunately, most of us have not independently analyzed the Biblical narrative even to question these age-old motifs that were delivered to us. By and large, we have abdicated that responsibility and have internalized the convictions of our associated religious system. The adherence to such positions is held tenaciously for our continued fellowship and promotion within any said body, and the inflexibility of those church systems has made it nigh impossible to inquire into these matters. The current inclination of those who wish to reconcile their historical or scientific views to the Biblical narrative has inadvertently discredited the authority of all scripture due to an erroneous motif and has earned Christianity the ridicule it rightly deserves.

Notwithstanding, the truth can not be discredited; it is only the proponents of such faulty systems themselves that bear the mark of sectarianism. Unfortunately, in the world of religious relativism, the truth is dismissed with a broad brush of ecclesiastical skepticism. We will now endeavor to dispel some of the myths and misconceptions associated with the most significant passages of Holy writ contained in Genesis One.

As we approach the sensitive issues within this volume, let us heed to the admonitions of wise men that preceded us...*says Bishop Wordsworth, "men make God's word their non-word, or even the tempters word, and then scripture is used for our destruction instead of making us wise unto salvation" 1. Miscellanies, ii.17 (Farrar).*

F.W. Farrar further writes, "The misinterpretation of scripture must be reckoned among the greatest calamities of Christendom. It has been the source of crimes and errors that have tended to loosen the hold of the sacred writings the affection and veneration of mankind. Recall but for a moment the extent and deadliness of the evils for which texts of the Bible have been made the command and the excuse. Wild fanaticism, dark superstition, abject bondage, anti-nomian license, the burning hatred and the unbending obstinacy of party spirit- have they not in turn perverted the Scriptures to which they appealed?"

The History of Interpretation, F.W. Farrar p.39

A Word on Interpretation

Many acquainted with the history of Biblical interpretation acknowledge that the allegorical/metaphorical approach to reading the scriptures is not new. We do not (as some have inferred) practice or support the wholesale utilization of allegory to scripture by whim. A passage in question must fit into a well-established blueprint represented throughout the Bible to qualify for integration into a particular motif. Likewise, we elicit the pieces from the whole of scripture only as demanded by the passage. Torturing a self-appointed narrative into a text should never be practiced, but unfortunately, it has for thousands of years. The vain attempt to yield treasures from an obscure passage without the aid of well-established patterns usually ends up in an unrecognizable heap of gobbledygook. As the adage goes, *"A text without a context is only a pretext."*

"In this manner also we ought to interpret, not the clear by the obscure but the obscure by the clear, and to revere in its dark sayings the divine wisdom which sees all things always, but does not reveal all things at once...where no particular time is indicated, or where time-limitations are kept out of view, the figure may be allowed, and is, indeed, a happy illustration. But when the Lord says that certain events are to follow immediately after certain other events, let no interpreter presume to say that millenniums may come between. This is not "to interpret the obscure by the clear," but to obscure the clear by a misleading fantasy."

Biblical Hermeneutics, Milton Terry 1883p.497-498

Secret Knowledge

Gnosticism of a Christian variety arose in the second century. Its wayward underpinnings are found in the philosophical teachings of Plato. He planted the seeds of secret knowledge only the elite could comprehend. Its various forms have influenced religious, philosophical, and political movements for thousands of years. The most influential figure to early Christianity in this respect was Philo of Alexandria, Egypt. He was a lover of Greek philosophy devoted himself to the endorsement of all things Hellenic. The blending of Hellenism and Judaism produced Neo-Platonism.

"Judaism and Hellenism, so to speak, came into the closest contact in this celebrated metropolis of Egypt, and in their spiritual and intellectual mingling produced what came to be known as Neo-Platonism....Philo appears, at times, to assume or allow the literal sense of a passage, but his great aim is to exhibit the mystic depths of significance which lie concealed beneath the sacred words... He seems to entertain no conception of the historical standpoint of his author and to have no realistic or historical sense of the truthfulness or accuracy of the statements of Moses. He seizes upon chance expressions and incidental analogies as matters of great moment, and lugs in farfetched notions that are utterly foreign to the plain meaning of the text."
Biblical Hermeneutics, Milton Terry 1883 p.611

Philo almost single-handedly transformed the Jewish world with his "hidden" Gnostic interpretations of the Torah. Plato was not his only major influence. The oral traditions of what later became the Zohar and the Talmud rendered the teachings of Moses of none effect (Mathew 15:5). Jesus and later, Paul recognized the error of this mystical teaching, and both fought it until their death. Gnostic teachings, be they Jewish or Christian, attain the same ends. Superficially, both systems acknowledge the Holy Scriptures with an assured lip service of devotion (a wink and a nod), but on the other hand, they only embrace and sponsor their clandestine narratives.

The oral "Talmudic" tradition formulated during the Babylonian exile. Its variety of Gnosticism emerged from Persia (Zoroastrianism). This oral tradition of the Jews stated that Moses received a secret oral law that was handed down from generation to generation. That unwritten law had absolutely no semblance to that of the Torah. This is the main bone of contention that inspired the strife between Jesus and his persecutors.

"Judaism considers what the Bible actually says as the outer "shell", and as we know, shells are meant to be discarded. Maimonides wrote concerning the Bible, "In every word which has a double sense, a literal one and a figurative one , the plain meaning as valuable as silver and the hidden meaning still more precious...For Rabbi Nahmanides, (thirteenth century) the plain text of the Bible was merely "an accommodation to the ordinary human mind."
Judaism Discovered, Michael Hoffman p.283

Judaism acknowledges that its methods of interpretation are emulated throughout the Christian world. Judaism's adaptation of Biblical numerology ascribes significance to words through their repetition and also through an ascribed mystical value to each letter that would yield some cryptic significance. Hidden narratives are fashioned through this method as it obfuscates the plain sense of the passage. This type of methodology typically breeds a plethora of implications, a smorgasbord of inferences that induces a form of mysticism in our midst. The Judaism of today is essentially Pharisaical or Orthodox Judaism. "It teaches that the text of the Bible when taken literally is misleading or erroneous. While there are 70 "faces" to the Talmud and the Kabbalah, there are "padres" four major levels of understanding the Old Testament according to the Rabbis."

1. The literal meaning of a verse or passage
2. The Aggadic or allegorical level
3. Midrashic and Talmudic admonitory and legal level
4. The magical; the level of Kabbalistic esoteric gnosis."

***Fishbane, "Jewish Biblical Exegesis; Presuppositions and Principles,"
In scriptures in the Jewish and Christian Traditions (University of Denver, 1982) page**

When the plain meaning of a word as "soon" is tortured into the conventional notion of thousands of years, one only wonders where this misbegotten strategy established its legitimacy in the world of Biblical exegesis. How do they mangle "a day is with the Lord is as a thousand years and a thousand years as one day" to create an ambiguous measuring stick to counter the charges of their fraudulent prophetic timekeeping?

..... "But they paid him(Aqiba) the yet higher compliment of adopting the whole of his amazing system. He taught them, and even Christians appear to have sanctioned his views- that "as the hammer divides fire into many sparks, so every verse of scripture has many explanations."

The History of Interpretation 1886 F.W. Farrar p.73

....These tactics should be exposed for what they are, and those who resort to such abuses challenged.

From the days of Philo, we have a great cast of characters, men of renown lionized and adored for their particular contribution to the general body of literature about Biblical interpretation. Much of what we have today by way of the strangest creeds emanated from their pens. That which Philo introduced through his wayward misuse of allegory was replicated in spirit by these so-called "Church Fathers." St. Clement of Rome, Barnabas, Justine Martyr, Irenaeus, Clement of Alexandria, Origen, Jerome, and Augustine were among that venerated body. Their heavy-handed ways of forging a narrative tailor-made to suit their time and circumstances should be apparent, but when the occasion arises, they are summoned from antiquity to resolve the more important doctrinal issues of our time. Many are not aware that few were fluent in Hebrew and were ill-prepared to embark upon the important work they attempted to accomplish. They eschewed anything that emulated a Judean creed or tradition and went to great pains to distance their "system" from that of the Judean institutions.

"The church writers of the earlier ages were inundated with difficulties. It was not until the forth century that the cannon of the New Testament was lastly established; it was not until the sixteenth that the Cannon of even the Old

25

Testament was finally established... and the entire library of the thirty-nine books, which hardly any of the Fathers could read in the original, was appealed to as the final authority.... Without deep learning without linguistic knowledge, without literary culture, without any final principles either as to the sacred writings or the method by which they should be interpreted surrounded by Paganism, Judaism and heresy of every description, and wholly dependent upon a faulty translation, the earliest Fathers and Apologists add little or nothing to our understanding of scripture. They are not to be blamed for decencies, which were inevitable. They could not transcend the resources of the days in which they lived... Their acquaintance with the Old Testament is incorrect, popular and full of mistakes; their scriptural arguments are baseless; their exegesis - novel in application only- is a chaos of elements unconsciously borrowed from Philo, and on the other from Rabbis and Kabbalists...The only bible used by the Apostolic Fathers was the Septuagint; and they rely upon its supposed inspiration even when it differs widely from the original Hebrew." **The History of Interpretation by F.W, Farrar pp. 164-165**

The Double Sense: Double Trouble

One of the greatest exploitations of Biblical interpretation is the use of a double sense in deciphering the meaning of scripture. The practice allows an otherwise ill-equipped expositor the widest leverage for introducing imaginative accounts to a doctrinal discussion without the adherence to the intended Biblical narrative. The result of such an enterprise is disastrous.

"Hence, has arisen not only the doctrine of a double sense, but of a threefold and a fourfold sense, and the rabbis went so far as to insist that there "mountains" of sense in every word of scripture. We may readily admit that the scriptures are capable of manifold practical applications; otherwise they would not be so useful for doctrine, correction, and instruction in righteousness. (2Ttimothy 3:16) But the moment we admit the principle that portions of scripture contain an occult or second sense we introduce an element of uncertainty to the sacred volume, and unsettle all scientific interpretation....To say that words do mean a thing merely because they can be tortured into meaning it is the most dishonorable and dangerous way of handling scripture...."

*"Some writers have confused this subject by connecting it with the doctrine of type and antitype. The judgment of Babylon, or Nineveh, or Jerusalem, may, indeed, be a type of every other similar judgment, and is a warning to all nations and ages; but this is very different from saying that the language in which that judgment was predicted was fulfilled only partially when Babylon or Nineveh or Jerusalem fell and yet awaiting for its complete fulfillment....*It is a reprehensible abuse of language to say that the words immediately, or near at hand, or nearly at hand, mean ages hence, or after a long time. Such a treatment of the language of scripture is even worse than the theory of double sense." **Biblical Interpretation, Milton Terry pp. 493-496**

The misappropriation of scripture has had far-flung historical consequences that reached beyond the customary scope of Church affairs. When the Catholic Church conjoined with the state in Europe, the reckless abuse of Biblical authority took on the ghastly form of the Inquisition. The Inquisition was the infernal politico-apparatus of repression, hatred, and petty religiosity fueled with embezzled authority from the contrived notions of scriptural piety.

"In the days of her persecution, the Fathers of the church had taught mankind that "force is hateful to God;" but, in the days of her despotism, not only cursings and anathemas, but axes, the stakes, the gibbets, the thumbscrews, the racks, and all the instruments of torture kept in the dungeons of priests to deprave the heart of nations, and to horrify the world, were defended by scraps of texts and shreds of metaphor from the mercy-breathing parables of Christ."
The History of Interpretation, F.W.Farrar,1886 Macmillan, London p.41

The following portion of this text will be devoted to enumerating the proper tools needed in approaching the study of the ancient manuscripts we call the Bible.

Eschew the Tendency to Universalize Scripture

Before the advent of the industrial revolution, most Bible students understood and welcomed the Bible's lyrical, poetic, and metaphorical value. This does not mean that all scripture should be analyzed in this way. What it does indicate is that we should be able to identify the innate structure of the passages accurately to facilitate their proper function within the realm of holy writ. The explosion of science-oriented industrial age not only changed the social mores and traditions of its day but also realigned man's entire world view. This view also exerted a tremendous influence on Biblical analysis as well. Our world became a smaller place through the advances made in travel and communication. As a result, our world became more comprehensible and accessible. Thus, our commerce, education, politics, and biblical exegesis became international and universal in scope. Inadvertently, the broad brush of universalism exerted its influence on Biblical teaching that still is with us to this day. Much of the criticism we have received for our prophetic view of Genesis One originates from the adherents of that same universal point of view. Under closer appraisal, we find that the Bible did not have that perspective. We must remember that the Word has communicated to the Near Eastern Bedouin in Paleo-Hebrew expressions nonexistent in the Modern Hebrew of our day. Two basic Historical realities arise from the sacred text:

1. The recipients of the Word had a limited world view (local, tribal)

2. The written Hebrew language expresses itself in concrete terms as opposed to the Western idioms inundated with adjectives and expressive terms to define words.

 Beware: Culture and Language Determine Our Ability or Inability to Interpret

"In fact, there is a kind of symbiotic relationship between the texts and interpretations: it is not simply a one- way street in which texts yield their meaning, but two- way street in which the meaning that one brings to a text in part determines how the text is read and understood. Some literary theorists have gone even farther, arguing that the basic assumptions, values, and desires (both conscious and unconscious) that readers bring to a text determine its meaning. In this view, the meanings of the texts are never self- generating, but are necessarily forged

by living and breathing human interpreters who are bound by to an intricate network of social, cultural, historical and intellectual contexts, contexts that affect both who a person is and how he or she will "see" the world at large including the texts within it. According to these theorists, this nexus of factors does more than influence the way texts are interpreted: it actually produces interpretations."

The Orthodox Corruption of Scripture, Bart D. Ehrman first ed. P 29-. 30

The struggle that many have with Genesis One is due to faulty conclusions arrived at by the propagators of cosmic view. Inadvertently, the verity and focus of scripture maligned by the proponents of such a view, and its impracticable assumptions have held the truth hostage. The institutionalization of this influence is apparent in every quarter of Christendom. As a result, countless millions have abandoned the Bible and its teachings.

Interpretation by the Onion

The traditional cosmic view of Genesis One fails in two ways:

1. Structure

2. Presentation

We say this because of the traditional narrative presents itself in a linear (as one reads a novel). As a result, its historical and prophetic rhythms are not in sync with one other. Thus it communicates an incoherent view of the Bible and its purpose. A good illustration of Biblical configuration would be that of an onion; one layer of skin laid upon another in a cyclical orientation (as a wheel within a wheel). Yes, we have many details of rigorous truth at our disposal, but they are not as cohesive as we lead ourselves to believe. Those well-meaning institutions dispense their homespun narratives while we humbly suppress our privately held reservations. The result is invariably a collective internalization of their pre-packaged agenda

Additional Tools of Interpretation

Another component the Western mind should consider when reading Hebraic literature is the unique way the prose and poetry conveyed conveys its message. Yes, although we may be reading the KJV, we are effectively reading Hebrew literature translated into the English language, and much lost by our inability to recognize the rhythms of thought produced by Hebrew prose and poetry. An example of this is called "Hebrew Parallelism."

*1. *Hebrew parallelism; it expresses one idea in two or more different ways. A great amount of the O.T. is poetry. All of Psalms and Proverbs are Hebrew poetry, Genesis is full of poetry. This is why the Torah was sung for easy*

memorization. Rabbis believed that if something is worth saying, it is worth repeating. Much of what is in the Bible is repeated in various ways it is called saying beautifully. *

*Referenced from The ancient Hebrew Research Center website www.ancienthebrew.org

If we read the Bible by its (native) Hebraic composition, we would immediately recognize its superior value as an interpretative tool. As with many Biblical applications, an idea is presented in a repetitive way to yield the various aspects of a central idea. (This also referred to as a chiastic literary expression) For example, Zechariah 12:1 emphasizes its central idea by using the words heaven, earth, and man in recounting covenant creation. These keywords are used synonymously in what we term "*prophecy speak*" because the creation of *heaven* and *earth* is, in effect, the creation of covenant *man*. These terms are fused interchangeably with an implied synoptic value to frame its subject matter. If we do not acknowledge this inherent value, the passage will lose its cohesiveness.

Zechariah 12:1

12:1 The burden of the word of the Lord for Israel, saith the Lord, which
1.*strecheth* forth the *heavens*, and
2. *layeth* the foundation of the *earth*, and
3. *formeth* the spirit of *man* within him.

Heavens = Earth = Man

Strecheth = Layeth = Formeth

The words, stretcheth, layeth, and formeth are also expressed synonymously in this rhythmic prophetic form. The same principles applied to the following passage where the aspects of the Godhead illustrated through the identification of words which express God's redemptive character. This method of writing frames the main subject with the repetition of its various components. The beauty of consolidating the teaching of one God in this passage dismisses any notion of three separate, distinct persons in a triune godhead.

Isaiah 44:6

Thus saith
1. **Jehovah**,
2. **king** of Israel, And
3. his **Redeemer**,
4. **Jehovah** of Hosts:
5. 'I [am] the **first**, and
6. I the **last**, And
7. besides Me, there is no **God**. YLT

Jehovah = King of Israel = Redeemer = Jehovah = First = Last = God

Another form of Hebrew parallelism is the use of negatives where two opposing ideas contrasted as evidenced in:

Proverbs 11:19-20

A1- Righteousness brings one to **life**

B1- Pursuit of evil things brings one to his **death**

B2- A twisted heart is an **abomination** to YHWH

A2- A mature path is his **pleasure**.

*Referenced from The ancient Hebrew Research Center website www.ancienthebrew.org

33

Genesis One and Two in Synoptic Creation

Genesis chapters One and Two are excellent examples of Hebrew parallelism in action. Genesis Two recounts creation with specifics not given in Genesis one. Chapter Two summarizes chapter one and draws attention to the main event in Genesis One, i.e., the covenant creation of man. Note that the order of creation in chapter two is not as in chapter one. The order of days 1-7 is not replicated in chapter two and for a good reason... it never was the intention of God to do so. Chapter one gives the macro-version of Creation. Chapter two gives the micro- version. It all boils down to the highlighting of various components of the narrative. The Torah illustrated a repetition of similar patterns, i.e., the stories in Exodus retold in various forms in Numbers and Deuteronomy. The same style of writing presents itself in First and Second Samuel, Kings, and Chronicles (the history of the Major and Minor Prophets live within its pages). The most apparent illustration for our position is that of the synoptic Gospels where parables and events are reiterated to reveal various facets of each particular message. We should also include the judgments of Revelation for good measure (i.e., the seals, trumpets, and bowls) because they communicate the same destructive narrative that yields a multidimensional showcasing of its respective components. In essence, the Biblical narratives are presented as a wheel within a wheel weaving an intricate, unfailing pattern as they divulge God's cohesive plan for the redemption of man from Genesis to Revelation.

If significant narratives are repeated and illustrated throughout the Bible, common sense tells us that we should also perceive the rudiments of those identical patterns commenced in Genesis One, the prototype where this methodological configuration begins. Well then, how do we identify these patterns in Genesis One? The correlations are easy to make once we can ascertain the pattern.

Genesis 1:2
And the earth was
a. *without form,*
b. and *void;* and
c. *darkness* was upon the face of the deep KJV

Genesis 1:6-7

And God said,
a. Let there be a firmament *in the midst* of the waters and
b.Let it *divide* the waters from the waters.

And God made the firmament and
c. *Divided* the waters which were under the firmament from the waters which were above the firmament: and it was so. KJV

In the following illustration, we note that three themes are reiterated in Genesis One: the light, waters, and land. These are the basic fundamental aspects developed in the "creation week." The illustrated repetition of these themes throughout the prophetic text emphasizes similar themes. In other words, the components of covenant relationship follow the patterns of:
1.) Light (repentance)

2.) Separation (holiness)

3.) Land (The new creature; resurrection)

Day 1 light introduced > Day 4 the division of
Day and Night

Day 2 the waters divided > Day 5 life from the
waters

 Day 3 the land appears > Day 6 man and beast
emerge from the land or earth

The Seventh-day the Eternal Rest of Covenant Creation

This creation theme illustrated in the narrative of the deliverance of the Hebrews in Exodus.
The *revelation* of purpose through the preaching of Moses prompted the exodus or *separation* of the people from Egypt as baptized unto Moses in the Red Sea. As a result, they *emerged from the water* an emancipated people, a new creation.

The New Testament embodies these same basic tenets through the preaching of John the Baptist, the separation from sin, and the receiving of the Holy Ghost, and the completion of the new creature. This pattern is demonstrated over again with the Covenant imagery illustrated by the death burial and resurrection of Jesus Christ.

Ancient Tools for the Interpretation of the Old Testament

The Modern Hebrew

ז ט ס'ה ו א ד/פ מ מ צ ד ל ח ן ע י כ ק ג ב נ ש

As we have previously stated, the earlier interpreters of scripture were ill-equipped for the enormous task set before them. They did so through the Greek manuscripts of the Septuagint, a flawed translation rife with faulty assertions. Their lack of knowledge of Hebrew and its ancient culture also proved to be a major weakness for these men.

"The Seventy (the Septuagint) had not realized that the necessity for absolute faithfulness, which we now regard as the first duty of every translator. Excellent as their version is, as a whole, it is in many details faulty, and it is full of intentional as well as of unintentional departures from the meaning of the original."
Milton Terry the History of Interpretation p.119 (1883)

"Thus, Judaism was introduced into the literature of the world, and its doctrines were popularized. On the other hand, however, it innocently led to a mistaken view of the

Judean Law, becoming in a measure a false prophet, promulgating errors in the name of God. The difficulty of translating the Hebrew into the Greek, a radically different language, at no time an easy task, was greatly increased at that period for the want of exact knowledge of Hebrew, and the true nature of Judaism which made it impossible for the translator always to render correctly the sense of the original. Moreover, the Greek text was not so carefully guarded, but that, from time to time, arbitrary emendations might have been introduced.
H. Graetz, History of the Jews p.513 vol.1 1891

We believe that deeper knowledge of the ancient Hebrew language is essential for uncovering a truer sense concerning what the Old Testament has to offer. For the clarification of the texts we study, we lean heavily upon the Early Semitic Script dated over 3,500 years ago. The reason for this is because each letter in that alphabet has an acknowledged interpretive assessment (we do not ascribe a mystic application of numerology, arbitrary values, or so-called Bible codes.) These interpretive appraisals were instituted thousands of years ago and are not to be subjected o the whims of modern surmising.

This method is the norm from the Near to Far Eastern languages, whether they are Phoenician, Ancient Hebrew, Egyptian, or Mandarin. The essential component within a word from these cultures lies in the association of its letters portrayed as pictures with their assigned interpretive value. The English language is not so; an "a" does not have intrinsic interpretive value in and of itself. Only when it is allied with other letters or phrases does the letter "a" ascertain its worth as it functions within a word, phrase, or sentence.

The "Ideographic" View of Paleo Hebrew

Early Semitic

Ideographic: Ideas conveyed through the depiction of symbols. The concreteness of Ancient Hebrew and its unique expressions derived from the culture that birthed it into existence. Its archaic terminology originates from a primitive Beduin/ Nomadic culture. The language reflects the basic needs and activities of those nomads who wandered the Near East before the philosophies of Plato and Zoroaster arose to influence their progeny.

When one reads a Biblical account in its ancient cultural setting, we immediately grasp the impractical task of relating its values into our own Western culture of nuances, philosophical musings, and meandering inferences. O the simplicity and candor of Hebraic yearnings; its conspicuous motives, forthright and without apology! Truly, the East does not meet the West, as they are divergent and resist amalgamation at every quarter. We must embrace the Near East in its primal setting and reacquaint ourselves with its unvarnished purity of expression and its proliferation of poetic imagery.

The coalescence of language and culture yields an undeniable imprint that is always implicitly understood by all those nurtured within their particular social stratum. Thus, our Western world view is akin to the proverbial nose on our face; it is very difficult to grasp the fact that we are missing the boat in the 21st Century about such far-removed ancient texts.

To illustrate our point, we will contrast a few Hebrew definitions for your edification. These concepts should demonstrate the great difficulty translators have had in rendering Hebrew in the English language. The word anger would be meaningless to the Ancient Hebrews because the word does not relate to their cultural experience. The expression, "flaring of the nostrils" would be immediately recognized by the Ancient Ones. Why would scribes pick the word anger to translate the "flaring of the nostrils?" The answer is simply a cultural one; we are not familiar with that term. Therefore the word anger is used. The Strong's Concordance integrated the proper term, but the KJV opted for the word anger...

Anger: The flaring of the side as in the sides of a ravine. A narrow ravine where the walls press the
nostrils in anger. Moreover: Greater in addition to something else in the sense of passion. [Aramaic only] [freq. 297] |kjv: anger, wrath, face, nostrils, nose, angry.

Anger:
OT:639 [a^ **'aph** (a); from OT:599; properly, the nose or nostril; hence, the face, and occasionally a person; also (from the rapid breathing in passion) ire:

KJV - anger (-gry), + before, countenance, face, + forbearing, forehead, + [long-] suffering, nose, nostril, snout, X worthy, wrath.

(Biblesoft's New Exhaustive Strong's Numbers and Concordance with Expanded Greek-Hebrew Dictionary. Copyright © 1994, 2003, 2006 Biblesoft, Inc. and International Bible Translators, Inc.)

Life:
1171) HhY) ac: **Live** : **Stomach** ab: **Life:** When the stomach is empty one is famished and weak and when it is filled one is revived. This organ is seen as the life as an empty stomach is like death but a revived stomach is life

"This word is usually translated as life but in one place, Job 38:39, this word is best translated as "stomach"; "Can you hunt the prey of the lion or fill the **stomach** *of the young lion?". From this, we see that life to the Ancient Hebrew is related to a full stomach."*

Jeff A. Benner, Ancient Hebrew Lexicon of the Bible

Job 38:39

39 Wilt thou hunt the prey for the lion? or fill the **appetite** of the young lions, KJV

Function

"Hebrew thought is more concerned with function whereas our Greco-Roman thought is more concerned with appearance. How would you describe a pencil? You would probably describe it as "long, yellow with a pointed end." Notice how we like to use adjectives to describe objects. However, in Hebrew thought, verbs are used much more commonly, and a pencil would be described as something you write with, a description of its function rather than its appearance. When we read the Biblical text we are constantly creating a mental image of what the text is describing. However, the original author is not describing an image of appearance – but an image of function...and this is how you aught to make it, the length of the vessel is three hundred cubits long, fifty cubits wide and thirty cubits high. Is this description telling us what the ark looked like? Not at all. It describing its function by telling us that ark is very large and capable of transporting a very large load of animals"

Jeff Benner, The Living Words Volume one, p.4

Genesis 1:26 (raw unedited text)

עַל־הָאָרֶץ הָרֹמֵשׂ הָרֶמֶשׂ וּבְכָל הָאָרֶץ וּבְכָל וּבַבְּהֵמָה הַשָּׁמַיִ◌ֽם וּבְעוֹף

and~ he~ will~ Say "Elohiym [*Powers*]"we~ will~ Do Human in~ Image~ us like~ Likeness~ us and~ he~ did~ Rule in~Swimmer the~ Sea~ s and~ in~ Flyer the~ Sky~ s2 and~ in~ Beast and~ in~ All the~ Land and~ in~ All the~ Treader the~ Tread~ ing(ms) Upon the~ Land

Genesis **1:26 (Edited text)**

and "Elohiym [*Powers*]" said, we will make a human in our image like our likeness, and he will rule in the swimmers of the seas and in the flyers of the sky and in the beast and in all of the land and in all of the treaders treading upon the land…

Genesis 1:26

26 And God said, Let us make man in our image, after our likeness: and let them have dominion over the fish of the sea, and over the fowl of the air, and over the cattle, and over all the earth, and over every creeping thing that creepeth upon the earth.

(Raw unedited text)

Genesis 1:27
and~ he~ will~ Fatten "Elohiym [*Powers*]" At the~ Human in~ Image~
him in~ Image "Elohiym [*Powers*]"he~ did~ Fatten At~ him Male and~
Female and~ he~ will~ Fatten At~them

Genesis 1:27 (edited text)
and "Elohiym [*Powers*]" fattened the human in his image, in the image of "Elohiym [*Powers*]" he fattened him, male and female he fattened them,

Genesis 1:27

27 So God created man in his image, in the image of God created he him; male and female created he them.
KJV

Mandarin, its *ideographic characters,* and Noah's Flood

Mandarin is an ancient Chinese language that is approximately 4,500 years old. It is the only ancient language that still functions in its unique ideographic narrative. The primary disposition of this ancient language is to tell its story through its images. Chinese Mandarin tells the story of early Genesis uniquely. Given that this language adopted in the remoteness of the Far East and its contents written 2,500 years before the advent of Christianity, its trustworthiness as an ancient witness to Genesis can hardly impinge. As with the Paleo Hebrew, Mandarin develops each of its words by associating its symbols with one another under the auspices of a root symbol. The methodical alignment of these symbols radiates its message in an identifiable narrative that is extremely concrete in its presentation and mostly devoid of the ambiguity of its Western counterpart.

"Our Chinese friend was embarrassed that he had, at that time, too little scientific persuasive evidence to substantiate the Genesis narrative of beginnings. He himself had always accepted it by faith — simply as the

Word of God. He wrestled with the problem for days until something that he had observed in a footnote of a Mandarin textbook used by a missionary came to mind. The character, two meaning boat, had been analyzed as follows: a vessel; eight; and mouth or person. A comment followed that, interestingly, Noah's ark, the first great boat, had just eight passengers:

Noah and his wife, with his three sons and their wives. "If this is not a mere happenstance, there should be other Biblically relevant characters," reasoned Kang. Quickly he wrote down the character for to create , and was astonished as he analyzed the components in this figure for the first time: is dust or mud; a mouth; the small downward stroke to the left of indicates movement or life; and means able to walk. The text in Genesis 2:7 came to his mind. "Then the Lord God formed man of dust from the ground, and breathed [with his mouth] into his nostrils the breath of life, and man became a living being" (not a baby but an adult,

Nelson, Ethel R. (1979-08-01). The Discovery of Genesis (Kindle Locations 73-83). Concordia Publishing House. Kindle Edition. *able to walk).*

boat

vessel

The leftmost character means "ship" or "vessel."

eight

The upper righthand character is the Chinese number "eight."

mouth

The bottom left hand character is the word for "mouth" or "person." The first boat mentioned in the Bible is Noah's ark. Just how many people or "mouths" were aboard this ship or vessel? Genesis 7:13 tells us: *"In the selfsame day entered Noah, and Shem, and Ham, and Japheth, the sons of Noah, and Noah's wife, and the three wives of his sons with them, into the ark."* So Noah's ark was a ship or a vessel with eight people. Yet the Chinese language -- predating the Hebrew in which the Old Testament was written by at least 700 years -

- records this fact in perfect detail.

The word "covet" or "desire" pictures a woman making a decision between two trees. Genesis 2:8-9 shows us that there were two significant trees side by side in the garden from which to choose. The woman made a wrong choice as we are told in :

Genesis 3:6.

林 + 女 = 婪
trees   *woman*   *desire, covet*

The Discovery of Genesis : How the Truths of Genesis Were Found Hidden in the Chinese Language by C. H. Kang, Ethel Nelson

As with all literary translations, the Bible incurs a great loss in translation, even when the greatest moral and intellectual efforts exerted. To compound the problem, we have neglected to access the value of the Ancient pen that yields its secrets while our Western Neo-Platonic world view has only served to impede our efforts to get to the bottom of things. The tools of the recent past have not served us well; therefore, we strive to remain faithful to the text as portrayed.

"Greek thought views the world through the mind (abstract thought) ancient Hebrew thought views the world through the senses (concrete thought). Concrete thought is the expression of concepts and ideas that can be seen, touched, smelled, tasted or heard. All five senses are used when speaking, hearing, writing and reading the Hebrew language. An example of this can be found in Psalms 1:3:

3. And he shall be like a tree planted by the rivers of water, that bringeth forth his fruit in his season; his leaf also shall not wither; and whatsoever he doeth shall prosper. KJV

"In this passage the author expresses his thoughts in concrete terms such as tree, streams of water, fruit and leaf. Abstract thought is the expression of concepts and ideas that are abstract in ways that cannot be seen, touched, smelled, tasted or heard. Examples of abstract thought can be found in: Psalms 103:8:

8 The Lord is compassionate and gracious, slow to anger, and plenteous in mercy. KJV"

"The words compassionate, gracious, anger, and love are abstract words, ideas that cannot be experienced by the senses. Why do we find these abstract words in a passage of concrete thinking Hebrews? Actually, these are abstract English words used to translate the original Hebrew concrete words. The translators often translate this way because the original Hebrew makes no sense when literally translated into English."

The Language of Parables, Dreams, Songs, and Allegory

What one must realize is that a great portion of Holy Writ expressed in what we call "word pictures." The New Testament records in Mathew 13:34 that Jesus preached exclusively in a parabolic manner (as was consistent with the traditions of those who preceded him). Expositors who insist on the "literal sense" of interpretation deny for themselves and all posterity the true richness and depth of what the text has to offer them. This all amounts to a cultural bias that disallows the movement of inspiration intended for its audience.

"It aught not shake our confidence in God's word to discover that he has given it so largely in imaginary pictures, in magnificent framework of embellished traditions, ravishing poetry, delightful allegory, suggestive parables, memorial dreams, and symbols of imperishable significance. The fullness and completeness, as well as the transcendent excellence of the revelations contained in this long series of divine communications are a convincing witness that the holy men of old wrote as they were moved by the Spirit of God. **Biblical Apocalyptics, M. Terry 1898 p.17**

An important tool: The value of recognizing audience relevance

An invaluable tool that is eschewed by most Biblical exegetes is the common-sense recognition of audience relevance. Audience relevance occurs when an audience receives an expectation through the teaching of Jesus, his Apostles, or the written Word. The expectation is framed in such a way not misunderstood for other persons, places, or distant times. Case in point: Mathew 24 depicts the dire warnings of Jerusalem's destruction and the end of the age of Law-keeping. The words you, ye, and your, are used seventeen times as Christ addresses his disciples. Evidence within scriptural context manifestly denotes a mixture of warnings and advice concerning what to do when certain events transpire. Only those who lived in the Ancient Judean world would have taken the words of Christ to heart, especially after he chronologically framed the events to occur within that generation...

1. "There shall not be left **here** one stone…."
2. "**Ye** shall hear of wars…."
3. "Then they shall deliver **you** up to be afflicted and shall kill **you** and **ye** shall be hated of all nations for my name's sake."
4. "When **ye** see the abomination of desolation as spoken by the prophet Daniel….."
5. "**Let them which be in Judea** flee unto the mountains…"
6. 'Let him which is on the housetop not come down…"
7. "Neither let him which is in the field …."
8. "Pray **ye** that **your** flight be not in the winter neither on the **Sabbath day**…"
9. "Then if any man say unto **you** here is Christ

   or there believe it not…"

10. "Behold I have told **you** before …"

11. "Wherefore if they shall say unto **you**, behold he is in the desert..."
12. "So likewise ye when **you** shall see these things, know that it is near even at the door...."
13. "Verily I say unto **you** this generation shall not pass, till all these things be fulfilled...."
14. "Watch therefore : for **ye** know not the hour **your** lord doth come...."
15. "Therefore be **ye** also ready for in such an hour as **ye** think not the son of man cometh.
16. "Verily I say unto **you**, that he should make him ruler over all of his goods."

"The counsels and admonitions were addressed to the disciples. They, and not men of subsequent generations were to see the signs by which they might know that he was nigh, even at their doors. What peoples of other lands and future times might see might see and know is nothing to the purpose in this context.

Biblical Apocalyptics M. Terry 1998 p. 243

A Contrast of Culture through their Words

We will now furnish a few examples of how verbal and cultural disparity has made it almost impossible to achieve a suitable interpretation of Holy Writ. As previously stated, the concreteness of Hebraic scripture diminished through the proliferation of Westernized perception and translation within biblical texts. We have provided a comparison of words below in an attempt to contrast the distinctions between the depiction of English words in the KJV and the definition of those words in the Greek and

Hebrew, respectively. For a correlation of meaning. We utilize the Septuagint. The Old and New Testaments were both written in Greek; thus, the equivalent significance of those Greek words utilized to analyze the Hebrew.

*An example is the Greek word πιστις (pistis, Strong's Grk. #4102), which means "faith," an

intellectual acceptance of what is true, a very abstract term. This Greek word is the translation of the Hebrew אמונה (emunah, Strong's Heb. #530), which literally means firm, securely fixed in place1*

Benner, Jeff (2011-06-05). New Testament Greek to Hebrew Dictionary (Kindle Locations 154-157). Ancient Hebrew Research Center. Kindle Edition.

And saying the time is fulfilled, and the kingdom of God is at hand: repent ye, and believe the gospel. (Mark 1:15, KJV)

KJV	Grk #	Heb #	Translation
Time	2540	4150	Appointed time
Fulfilled	4137	4930	A Nail (secured)
Kingdom	932	4438	Empire
God	2316	430	Elohiym
Hand	1448	5066	Draw near
Repent	3340	5162	Breathing deeply
Believe	**4100**	**539**	**Support**
Gospel	2098	1309	Good news

Romans 10:16

16 But they have not all obeyed the gospel.

For Esaias saith, Lord, who hath believed our report? KJV

Hebrews 11:1

Now faith (support) is the substance of things hoped for, the evidence of things not seen. KJV

In the familiar verse cited above, faith = substance = evidence because faith is the product of observable support. Faith has dimension, substance, and evidenced through actions that demonstrate its importance. Thus, the Hebraic view dispels the abstract misapprehension of the elusive definition of this word. Its meaning reaches far beyond conceptual, emotional, and theoretical surmising. Faith becomes information (the Word) performed. Without its supportable, observable evidence, the existence of faith should be highly suspect. Thus, faith without works is dead.

Faith:
NT:5287 **hupostasis** (hoop-os'-tas-is); from a compound of NT:5259 and NT:2476; a setting under (**support**), i.e. (figuratively) **concretely, essence**, or abstractly, **assurance** (objectively or subjectively):

(Biblesoft's New Exhaustive Strong's Numbers and Concordance with Expanded Greek-Hebrew Dictionary. Copyright © 1994, 2003, 2006 Biblesoft, Inc. and International Bible Translators, Inc.)

Mark 1:14-15

14 Now after that John was put in prison, Jesus came into Galilee, preaching the gospel of the kingdom of God,

15 And saying, The time is fulfilled, and the kingdom of God is at hand: repent ye, and believe (support) the gospel. KJV

Creation: A lack of function not a lack of material origins

The creation of six days produced what John Walton called functionaries: Sun, Moon, Stars, Winged Fowl, Living Creatures, Cattle, Creeping Things, Beasts of the Field, Fish of the Sea, and Man. As we view these themes recurring in scripture, we will begin to appreciate how these multifaceted images repeat similar narratives with unique precision. Their *function* is as follows: To divide, gather, give light, rule, multiply, eat, subdue, bring forth, make or to form, to have dominion.

*"Instead of offering a statement of causes, Genesis One is offering a statement of how everything will work according to God's purposes. In that sense, **the text looks to the future** (how this cosmos will function for human begins with God at its center), **rather than into the past** (how God brought material into being.")*
John Walton The Lost World of Genesis One p.117

Walton accurately documented that the narrative of Genesis One does not exclusively consign itself to a set of historical events of the past but also the future. He recognizes its organic associations through a discernable pattern of divine organization in the balance of scripture. In other words, the nature of creation is not a lack of a material origin but covenantal function as its themes developed throughout the Bible. Jurgen Moltman echoes a similar view.

"The Bible, to some extent offers the idea that creation is ongoing and dynamic". ." **Jurgen Moltmann, God in creation : a new Theology of Creation and the Spirit of God (Harper & Row 1985) pp.226-27**

Theologian Jurgen Moltmann believes that God's creative work is not a static work of the past, but it is dynamic as it continues in the present and into the future.

Genesis 1:2 depicts a state of dysfunction rather than a state of non- material existence. Transforming the imagery of verse two from a non- functioning state to one that functions is at the heart of the Bible story. This view radically contradicts the prevailing views of a Universal creation. The lack of function in Genesis 1:2 is its central theme, not its lack of material origin.

Genesis 1:2

2 And the earth was without **form, and void; and darkness was upon the face of the deep.** And the Spirit of God moved upon the face of the waters.

Genesis1:2

2. And the land had _existed in confusion_ and _was unfulfilled_ and darkness was upon the face of the deep sea, and the wind of Elohiym was much fluttering upon the face of the water.

Jeff A. Benner, **Mechanical Translation of the Book of Genesis.**

In essence, Genesis 1: 2 is the preamble to the first day of creation without which the balance of creation would be unlikely. Genesis 1:2 functions as its initiator through the "fluttering" of the Spirit upon the deep of an unregenerated mass of humanity. The word _rachaph (move),_ according to Gesenius, does not take a Western approach to the word as Strong's' Concordance does. He understood its organic implications and did so in great detail. It virtually alters the historically held narrative that the Spirit of God somehow glides or hovers over the waters. Its true narrative is so much more endearing when taken into account how the Love of God portrayed as he initiated a loving covenant relationship with his people.

OT:7363 רָחַף **rachaph** (raw-khaf'); a primitive root; to brood; by implication, to be relaxed: *KJV* - flutter, move, shake.

(Biblesoft's New Exhaustive Strong's Numbers and Concordance with Expanded Greek-Hebrew Dictionary. Copyright © 1994, 2003, 2006 Biblesoft, Inc. and International Bible Translators, Inc.)

Verse three complies with the narrative of this non-functioning theme through a reversal of its condition by the addition of light. After this, God declared that his work was _good._ The Western expression of the word "good" is ambiguous as it fails to depict the work of God in verse. The proper Hebraic illustration should be the word *function.* It is "good" because now it functions. God's action was not morally good; it was good because it now functions.

Genesis 1:3-4

and "Elohiym [Powers]" said, light exist, and light existed and "Elohiym [Powers]" saw the light given that it was _functional_ and "Elohiym [Powers]" made a separation between the light and the darkness

Jeff A. Benner, Mechanical Translation of the Book of Genesis

Genesis 1:3-4

3 And God said, Let there be light: and there was light.

4 And God saw the light, that *it was* good: and God divided the light from the darkness. KJV

There was no man

The restatement of creative activity portrayed in the second chapter of Genesis verse five. The lack of function in the expression," not a man to till the ground," is reiterated throughout scripture in various forms and is readily recognizable through its similar content. The ground or "adamah" needs cultivation, nurturing and oversight, a theme profoundly represented in the parables of Jesus and the prophetic metaphors in the writings of the Prophets. Whether it is working the Garden of Eden, the adamah, the vineyard, the land flowing with milk and honey, or the Kingdom of God, its imagery expresses the same type of concern. Genesis One is not exempt from this pattern; it is its initiator.

Genesis 2:5

5 And every plant of the field before it was in the earth, and every herb of the field before it grew: for the Lord God had not caused it to rain upon the earth, and ***there was not a man (Adam) to till the ground (Adamah)***. KJV

Genesis 2:5

And of all the shrubs of the field *before existing in the land* and all of the herbs of the field *before* springing up given that "YHWH" of "Elohim" did not make it precipitate upon the land and without a human TO SERVE THE GROUND.

Jeff A.Benner, Mechanical Translation of the Book of Genesis.

Matthew 15:12-14

12 Then came his disciples, and said unto him, Knowest thou that the Pharisees were offended after they heard this saying?

13 But he answered and said, *Every plant, which my heavenly Father hath not planted, shall be rooted up.*

14 Let them alone: they be blind leaders of the blind. And if the blind lead the blind, both shall fall into the ditch. KJV

The English translation of the Bible obscures the close relationship between the words "Adam" and "ground." The relationship between "Adam" and "Adamah" (ground) is arresting as viewed through its ancient script.

"Adam is rendered as "red" as the color of the shedding of blood, dyed red, ruddy or person.
The "parent root) of both words is (דם) blood, the pictograph is a tent door moving back and forth . The ᴍis a picture of water and can represent any liquid especially blood. Combined these pictures mean "the moving back and forth of water" or "the moving back and forth of blood." Similarly, the grape plant takes water from the ground and moves it to the fruit where the water becomes the blood of the grape.
Ancient Hebrew Lexicon of the Bible Jeff A. Benner p.93

The lack of covenant functionaries in Genesis 2:5 compliments the need in Genesis 1:2 for an Adam to work the adamah (ground).

Genesis 2:5

5 And every plant of the field before it was in the earth, and every herb of the field before it grew: for the Lord God had not caused it to rain upon the earth, and *there was* **not a man** to till the ground. KJV

Both verses are expressing identical themes. **Isaiah 50:1-3** also uses the same expression as it conveys the crisis of covenantal indolence. Note the covenantal aspects of Genesis One as the Creation atrophies, as its functionaries (man, sea, fish, water, and the heavens) fail to fulfill their designated purposes.

No intercessor

Isaiah 50:1-3

50 Thus saith the Lord, Where is the bill of your mother's divorcement, whom I have put away? or which of my creditors is it to whom I have sold you? Behold, for your iniquitie,s have ye sold yourselves, and for your transgressions is your mother put away.

2 Wherfore, when I came, **was there no man**? When I called, was there none to answer? Is my hand shortened at all, that it cannot redeem? or have I no power to deliver? behold, at my rebuke I dry up the sea, I make the rivers a wilderness: their fish stinketh, because there is no water, and dieth for thirst.

3 I clothe the heavens with blackness, and I make sackcloth their covering.

Isaiah 59:15-16

15 Yea, truth faileth, and he that departeth from evil maketh himself a prey: and the Lord saw it, and it displeased him that there was no judgment.

16 And he saw that **there was no man**, and wondered that there **was no intercessor**: therefore his arm brought salvation unto him; and his righteousness, it sustained him. KJV

Isaiah 41:28-29

28 For I beheld, and *there was no man; even among them*, and there was no counselor, that, when I asked of them, could answer a word.

29 Behold, they are all vanity; their works are nothing: their molten images are wind and confusion. KJV

The frequent reference to the Garden of Eden as the archetypal ideal of covenantal life points to the fact that Adam in tending the Garden glorified God in his purpose of wholeness and functionality. This familiar allegory further develops its narrative in the following passage in Ezekiel adopted from Genesis One. Verse 33 owes its underpinnings to verse 2 of Genesis One as the words iniquities, wastes, and desolate are each utilized to exemplify the dysfunction of a pre-creation era. In the time of Ezekiel Israel, was undergoing a period of what some of us refer to as de-creation.

Ezekiel 36:33-35

33 Thus saith the Lord God; In the day that I shall have cleansed you from all your iniquities I will also cause *you* to dwell in the cities, and the wastes shall be builded.

34 And *the desolate land shall be tilled,* whereas it lay desolate in the sight of all that passed by.

35 And they shall say, This land that was desolate is become like the garden of Eden; and the waste and desolate and ruined cities *are become* fenced, *and* are inhabited. KJV

In Conclusion

To proceed effectively with this volume, we felt that it would be advantageous for the reader to be aware of the tools utilized by those of us who support the views contained herein. The hardened approaches to Biblical interpretation have consistently yielded narratives that are wholly contradictory if not downright confusing. These approaches have the imprint of man's Western initiative, but unfortunately, they lack the ancient Near Eastern author's attendant genius. Thus, the incessant groping, miscalculation, and wayward assumptions continue unabated with the same predictable patterns because the same old faulty devices used in analyzing Holy Writ. In essence, if we desire a more successful outcome, we must of necessity, implement a modification of our procedures. This poses an extraordinary methodological challenge for teaching this subject. The urge to rely upon the tools of yesteryear obscures the vision for what the Bible is attempting to transmit. Thus, a renewed enthusiasm for an alternate interpretive discipline will be essential if we are to negotiate the pitfalls of the old guard.

Chapter One

שָׁמַיִם Heaven and Earth אֶרֶץ

The Bible endeavors to depict the Heavens and Earth as the object of God's love and mercy within a form of writing foreign to the speculations of modern scholarship. In spite of its simplicity and sublime presentation, we have failed to perceive the principal motivation for the writing of the holy text. The notion that God would devote the initial statements of Genesis One as a first mention as a prototype addressing the creation of the universe is an utter mystery. We say this because the balance of what we call the Bible does not replicate that premise, i.e. a continuation of a cosmic narrative. What we do find depicted within its pages is a reoccurring theme of devastation and redemption beginning in the second verse of its text. Its function and purpose never veer from its objectives because all of scripture sustains a narrative of the care and wellbeing of the Heaven and the Earth.

"All interpretation of language, whether literal or symbolic, must proceed on fixed principles. "Such views imply that the Old Testament symbols are systematically introduced in the Apocalypse and also that they have a fixed and uniform meaning; and that we are not at liberty to interpret them in any random mode. They are settled and defined in terms, each having its uniform meaning. The Revelation must be viewed and interpreted in connection with its roots in Old Testament prophecy"
Imp..Biblical Dictionary

The essence of Covenant Creation is the instruction of the Biblical narrative from its inception as it endorses its ongoing themes developed through their preliminary expressions. Are we to relegate the heavens and the earth to merely a footnote in the history of man? Or will we honestly acknowledge that the objective of this divine depiction was to prophetically articulate the purpose of God's kingdom for the deliverance of covenant man?

There are more than a few Bible scholars that acknowledge the fact that the term, "Heaven and Earth," was used to refer to both the old kingdom ruled by Mt. Sinai and the new kingdom ruled by the Messiah; thus the terms "old heaven and earth and new heaven and earth" respectively.

"John never speaks of heaven in the abstract as modern Christians too commonly do. He never uses the name as a proper name, like the name of cities or kingdoms. In describing the introduction of the new economy instead of the old, <u>which were called by the prophets the heaven and the earth,</u> he calls it a new heaven which depicts the opening of the gospel age at the incarnation. But here, in the epistles to the churches (Revelation chapters.2 and 3), the Lord is speaking of what is already begun. Accordingly he speaks not of "heaven" but of "the heaven." And thus, through all the visions in which the seals, trumpets, and phials are exhibited, "the heaven,' is invariably spoken of. Inattention of this leads many Christians to explain away the employments in "the heaven" in Rev.Chapters 5 and 7as being "in heaven' and altogether secluded from the present life. This denudes the believers of the privileges and the promise contained in these." **The Apocalypse Translated andExpounded James Glasgow 1872p. 169**

As we journey through this volume, we will regularly utilize the idiom "Heaven and Earth" in its appropriate allegorical setting. The terms employed in a poetical or prophetic sense in most Biblical environments. Rarely are these terms used in the literal or natural sense. As the Bible unfolds, its creatures, life forms, mountains, hills, and valleys; fish and beasts are all animated before our eyes. Most students of scripture are not aware that this Biblical caricature of nature has inadvertently become a sort of comic book depiction nestled amid the most severe prophetic reprimands recorded in the Bible. One can only wonder if God gets infuriated with his cosmic creation as he proceeds to curse and destroy its majestic splendor through the prophecies of old.

The Christian world is currently anticipating a literal fulfillment of the prophecies concerning the destruction of this planet; i.e., the heavens with its stars, the sun, and our moon. Logically, that would also consist of every planet in our solar system because without a functioning sun, the planets would loose from their gravitational moorings and great planetary devastation would ensue. This does not seem logical when we consider the character of God, his justice, and his expressed covenantal intentions, as evidenced in the Word. The notion of planetary devastation is an alien concept to the Bible's Hebraic sentiments and its inherent traditions. The conventional modern Biblical narrative begins with a universal creation and concludes with its destruction. If this embodies the primary agenda of our faith, then we can only conclude that God is preoccupied with creating and judging the inanimate. We have little scriptural evidence as to why this would be his concern because biblical judgment is the penalty for the breaking of a living covenant. The cosmos is but an unresponsive mass of matter and is of little consequence to the Kingdom and its purposes.

On the other hand, if we would consider that the terms heaven and earth are but metamorphic terms for a covenant body without form and void....then its apparent reformation through the prophetic seven day week would serve to assign its devices to man's history throughout the ages.

God's dialogue with heaven and earth essentially begins in Genesis One as he restores function to a broken system. He decrees its frontiers and its patterns within a cosmological idiom intended for the covenantal apple of his eye. For those who dismiss this important element of the first mention, we will furnish hard evidence of its persistence throughout the sacred text. Please note the emotional and human characteristics ascribed to the imaging of heaven and earth.

Deuteronomy 32:1-2

32 *Give ear*, O ye heavens, and I will speak; and *hear, O earth*, the words of my mouth.

2 My doctrine shall drop as the rain, my speech shall distil as the dew, as the small rain upon the tender herb, and as the showers upon the grass: KJV

Jeremiah 2:12-13

12 *Be astonished*, O ye heavens, at this, and *be horribly afraid*, be ye very desolate, saith the Lord.

13 For my people have committed two evils; they have forsaken me the fountain of living waters, *and* hewed them out cisterns, broken cisterns, that can hold no water.

Isaiah 44:23

23 *Sing, O ye heavens*; for the Lord hath done *it*: *shout, ye lower parts of the earth: break forth into singing, ye mountains*, O forest, and every tree therein: for the Lord hath redeemed Jacob, and glorified himself in Israel. KJV

The perceived allusion to the supposed cosmic creation of Genesis 1:14 is very persuasive in the following passages, although as we will see, cosmology is not the focus of these expressions. Just as Jacob understood Joseph's dream as it depicted the sun, moon, and eleven stars in obeisance to him, this imagery also only speaks to the covenant economy. Even the heavens and the waters above the heavens must praise the name of the Lord....

Psalms 148:3-5

3 *Praise ye him*, sun and moon: praise him, all ye stars of light.

4 *Praise him*, ye heavens of heavens, and ye waters that *be* above the heavens.

5 Let them praise the name of the Lord: for he commanded, and *they were created.* KJV

The Song of Moses begins in the 32nd chapter of Deuteronomy. Its essential properties and prophetic destinations characterized in the book of Revelation, where the judgments of "the latter days" articulated by Saint John. We can see this by the reference to avenging the blood of his adversaries; a theme reverberated in passages such as Mathew 23 and Revelation 18. Please note that Deut. chapter 32: 44 says that the words of that song were delivered into the ears of the people. This substantiates our belief that the beginning of this address to the ears of heaven and earth in chapter 32:1 are the ears of the Commonwealth of Israel.

In verse 43, we should be read, "Rejoice, O ye nations, his people;" "and will be merciful unto his land, to his people." The conjunction *and* is italicized and obfuscates the association of nations as being synonymous with both his people and land (**Adam**ah O.T.127 Strong's).

Nations = his people   Land = his people

Deuteronomy 32:1, 43-44

1. Give ear, O ye heavens, and I will speak; and hear, O earth, the words of my mouth. KJV

43 Rejoice, O ye nations, *with* his people: for he will avenge the blood of his servants, and will render vengeance to his adversaries, and will be merciful unto his land, *(and)* to his people.

44 And Moses came and spake all the words of this song in the ears of the people, he, and Hoshea, the son of Nun. KJV

The Passing of Heaven and Earth

The prevailing misapprehension of the terms *heaven and earth* have held enormous ramifications regarding the position that the church has adopted in areas related to the study of Biblical prophecy. The ever awaited second coming of Christ imagined through a long-established litany of passages thought to be associated with a cosmological demise of the sun, moon, stars, heaven, and the earth. The reliance upon this cosmologically perceived verbiage restricts the interpretation to be contingent upon these same catastrophic events to confirm their ever-impending fulfillments. Thus, they say with great confidence, "The end is yet to come." Such confidence is as "one who leans upon a bruised reed," as was the admonishment of the king of Assyria to Hezekiah concerning the aid of Egypt. Such cosmic assurances quickly evaporate under closer scrutiny of the holy text.

Celestial eschatological patterns depict a people of the heavenly domain. They have been taken and formed out of the dust of the **adam**ah and have the **breath** (neshamah character or name) of their heavenly Father. Thus, heaven is their celestial city (New Jerusalem), and the earth is the place of their origin. The ladder that Jacob viewed in the visions of the night illustrated this principle as the heavenly host ascended and descended upon it. Jacob exclaimed, "How dreadful is this place! This is none other, but the house of God (Bethel), and this is the gate of heaven."

The visualization of heaven and earth enjoined in this way was interpreted by Jacob as the house of God. Thus we have heaven and earth defined as the house of God. The event generally acknowledged as the time of Jacob's conversion. Covenant man begins his journey of salvation with a revelation on this earthly sphere that initiates him into the heavenly realm. The covenantal birth alluded to in the dialogue between Jesus and Nicodemus powerfully portrays many of the aspects of Jacob's dream as Jesus spoke of the new covenant birth of water and spirit. Within that dialogue, verse 13 embedded as if out of nowhere, but its implications are recognizable; salvation for man is contingent upon the Son of man first descending and then ascending into heaven. He is, in effect, the ladder that joins heaven and earth, the house of God. The imagery does not end there because Jesus astounded Nathaniel in their initial meeting by making the same allusions to Jacob's ladder and the dialogue between Jesus and Nicodemus in John 1:47-51. It confirmed in Nathaniel that Jesus was truly, "the Son of God; the King of Israel."

John 3:13

13 and no one hath gone up to the heaven, except he who out of the heaven came down — the Son of Man who is in the heaven. YLT

John 1:47-51

47 Jesus saw Nathanael coming to him, and saith of him, Behold an Israelite indeed, in whom is no guile!

48 Nathanael saith unto him, Whence knowest thou me? Jesus answered and said unto him, Before that Philip called thee, when thou wast under the fig tree, I saw thee.

49 Nathanael answered and saith unto him, Rabbi, thou art the Son of God; thou art the King of Israel.

50 Jesus answered and said unto him, Because I said unto thee, I saw thee under the fig tree, believest thou? thou shalt see greater things than these.

51 And he saith unto him, Verily, verily, I say unto you, Hereafter ye shall see heaven open, and the angels of God ascending and descending upon the Son of man. KJV

Genesis 28: 11-12,16-17

11 And he lighted upon a certain place, and tarried there all night, because the sun was set; and he took of the stones of that place, and put *them for* his pillows, and lay down in that place to sleep.

12 And he dreamed, and behold a ladder set up on the earth, and the top of it reached to heaven: and behold the angels of God ascending and descending on it.

16 And Jacob awaked out of his sleep, and he said, Surely the Lord is in this place; and I knew it not.

17 And he was afraid, and said, *How dreadful is this place! this is none other but the house of God, and this is the gate of heaven.KJV*

Through careful analysis, we have gathered much evidence concerning the Biblical identity of heaven and earth. We endeavor to confirm its Hebraic role in the sacred text from its initial introduction in Genesis One to its passing and recreation in the book of Revelation. The import of the following remarks made by the Lord in Matthew 5 alluding to the heaven and earth are lost to the literalist, but to the Jews who anticipated the realized kingdom in their generation, it was a breath of fresh air. The main points that Jesus addresses in this text are the passing of the Law or the transition of the covenants. The word TILL (or until) in vs. 18 indicated a prophetic chronological destination *when* the constraints of Law are no longer required as it finds its fulfillment in the church. The words "jot and tittle" refer to the entirety of the Law, which remained intact TILL the covenantal transition of "Heaven and Earth." Thus, when the passing of Jerusalem, its Temple, and the Levitical Priesthood were accomplished; the consummation of the New Jerusalem, it's New Temple, and Priesthood came into its fulfillment. On the other hand, if we violate the sentiments of this account and superimpose a cosmic tragedy into its narrative, we inadvertently destroy the expectation of its first-century audience and force its anticipation into the 21st century.

Matthew 5:17-18

17 Think not that I am come to destroy the law or the prophets: I am not come to destroy, but to fulfil.

18 For verily, I say unto you, *Till* heaven and earth pass, one jot or one tittle shall in no wise pass from the law, *till all be fulfilled*. KJV

The Meek Shall Inherit the Earth

The Sermon on the Mount offers a preview of the New Testament prerequisites for admission and continued participation in the kingdom of God. Matt. 5 verses 3-8 depict the spiritual posture required to access its covenantal benefits. Its original text dictated from the Aramaic tongue and written in Geek, but its author Matthew was a Hebrew, and that influence is very much evident in the passage. The following six verses are written in the style of Hebrew parallelism. Its narrative frames the subject matter quite well as the kingdom embraced in a prescribed manner. The false narrative of the Church to inherit a kind of an earthly real estate in the future abrogates the text. (A good example of how one word is taken out of its Hebraic context to suit the whims of the status quo). In sentiment, inherit the _earth_ in verse five, synonymously agrees with its neighboring verses 3, 4, 6, 7, and 8. Verse 13 continues to employ the word _earth_ in its covenantal context by continuing to embody the same figurative values of verse five.

Matthew 5:3-8

3 Blessed are the poor in spirit: for theirs is _the kingdom of heaven._

4 Blessed are they that mourn: for they shall _be comforted_.

5 Blessed are the meek: for they shall inherit the _earth_.

6 Blessed are they which do hunger and thirst after righteousness: for they _shall be filled_.

7 Blessed are the merciful: for they shall _obtain mercy._

8 Blessed are the pure in heart: for _they shall see God_. KJV

¶ **13** Ye are the *salt of the earth*: but if the salt have lost his savour, wherewith shall it be salted? it is thenceforth good for nothing, but to be cast out, and to be trodden under foot of men. KJV

Many Bible students fail to rightly divide the placement of this passage in the New Testament portion of their Bibles. Technically, the Sermon on the Mount is chronologically before the crucifixion. Thus it should essentially be assigned to the Old Testament. The imagery of these prerequisites understood by some, but when they reflect upon, "The meek shall inherit the earth," they revert from its inherent symbolic properties to a literalized use of the word earth. As a result, the expectation of covenant life reduced to the fanciful notion of a revived planet with its formerly marginalized denizens now restored to some "earthly" blessing on the material plane. The obvious references made to "the kingdom of God' in this text are, in fact, directly tied to covenant earth (the land flowing with milk and honey). This faithful narrative is now totally abandoned for one of a cosmic renewal; thus, the "New Heaven and Earth" are colonized yet again with multitudes of resurrected believers in "glorified bodies." Regrettably, this narrative is believed by many Christians in spite of the admonitions of our Lord concerning the kingdom of God

(Luke 17:20-21)

Now having been questioned by the Pharisees as to when the kingdom of God was coming, He answered them and said, "The kingdom of God is not coming with signs to be observed; **21** nor will they say, 'Look, here *it is!*' or, 'There *it is!*' For behold, the kingdom of God is in your midst." NASU

Ye are the Salt of the Earth

On face value, the passages that we previously analyzed might seem awkward or even in some cases, downright absurd for the ancient culture. Notwithstanding, the adaptation of human features, emotions, and activities should alert us all to question their underlying objective. Most individuals who regularly study scripture experience uneasiness with the incongruity that these phrases present, especially when interpreted in such a glib manner. Something does not feel right about it, but we fail to address the situation because we have lacked the tools that are required to evaluate the materials at hand. Nevertheless, it is not a complicated endeavor, nor does it take a great deal of education to perceive these applicable patterns and objectives. Just as one has acquired the distorted views of the future destruction of the universe, one only needs to acknowledge the Bible's true form, style, and structure to make the necessary adjustments. Matthew 5:13 would fit well into the category of the bizarre if it were to be taken purely on its face value. Essentially, its narrative speaks of the continuation of the kingdom of God through the faithfulness of its constituents. Commentators generally acknowledge the spiritual implications of this passage, but they append a universal notion to the text by way of overreaching conclusions founded upon the modern presentation of the word earth. The inferred teaching that the church will return to a renovated globe inhabited by the Saints. The inheritance of a refurbished terah firma found a permanent home in the literalist/ universal crowd. Culturally speaking, the use of salt had great value in the ancient world as a preservative and as a means of exchange; By metaphorically alluding to covenant people like salt, the Lord depicted them as agents that sustain the kingdom of God. The strange notion that the Church would function as a guardian of the secular world, or earth as we know it, is absurd and has no place in sound Biblical narrative. The problems generated by misappropriating the significance of the word _earth_ reoccur when using the word _world _ in the same vein. _We will address this important facet of our discussion in a succeeding scriptural development entitled, "Ye are the Light of the World."

Matthew 5:13

¶ **13** Ye are _the salt of the earth_: but if the salt have lost his savour, wherewith shall it be salted? It is thenceforth good for nothing, but to be cast out, and to be trodden under foot of men. KJV

Mark 9:50

50 Salt *is* good: but if the salt have lost his saltness, wherewith will ye season it? Have salt in yourselves, and have peace one with another. KJV

Ye are the Light of the World

The expression "Ye are the salt of the earth" is immediately followed by the phrase, "Ye are the light of the world." These pronouncements of Christ to the Church infer its designated sphere of influence to be covenantal. Both expressions refer to the same subject: an autonomous constituency where the Church exerts its greatest influence…

Matthew 5:14-16

14 Ye are the light of the world. A city that is set on an hill cannot be hid.

15 Neither do men light a candle, and put it under a bushel, but on a candlestick; and it giveth light unto all that are in the house.

16 Let your light so shine before men, that they may see your good works, and glorify your Father which is in heaven. KJV

The book of Revelation also uses these words interchangeably as it accurately depicts the object of its commentary…

Revelation 3:10

10 Because thou hast kept the word of my patience, I also will keep thee from the hour of temptation, which shall come upon all the *world,* to try them that dwell upon the *earth*. KJV

The Three Worlds of Mathew 24

Matthew 24 accurately demonstrates the dyslexic verbal confusion caused by the misappropriation of the word "world" in some of the English translations of the Bible. The impulse for this digression is that the translators desired to maintain the narrative of future cosmic destruction of the entire planet and its solar system. Thus, we have a rendering of the scripture in Matt 24:3 as "what shall be the sign of thy coming, and of the end of the world?"

NT:165 **aion** (ahee-ohn'); from the same as NT:104; properly, an age; by extension, perpetuity (also past); by implication, the world; specially (Jewish) a Messianic period (present or future): **(Biblesoft's New Exhaustive Strong's Numbers and Concordance with Expanded Greek-Hebrew Dictionary. Copyright © 1994, 2003, 2006 Biblesoft, Inc. and International Bible Translators, Inc.)**

The prevailing view of that passage has inspired its anticipated notions of impending catastrophic judgment to be immediate with its dreadful message of the end of all things. The translators knew that the word *aion* properly translated should have been rendered "age," but that would have obscured the preferred narrative. Thus, the word "*world*" suited their ends as it has served their masters well by misleading us all with their good intentions. The blunder continues by the second usage of the word "world" in Mathew 24:21:

21 For then shall be great tribulation, such as was not since the beginning of the *world* to this time, no, nor ever shall be. KJV

In this second illustration, the proper Greek rendering of

this word is cosmos; however, attention is drawn to an assumed commencement of the planet and its life forms in Genesis One. Again this replicates the institutional bias of the translators who gently channel our perceptions into their prescribed conclusions. The term cosmos or *world* is used very often in the New Testament, predominantly referring to the Judean, religious, or political world of the time. Evidence of how the term "world" understood by its own faction documented by one of its most celebrated historians. Heinrich Graetz was the first to write a six-volume comprehensive history of the Jewish people. In Volume I page 422, Graetz writes:

"Not only was Simon the Just recognized in his office of high- priest as head of the community and the Supreme Council, but he was also the chief teacher in
the house of learning. He inculcated the maxim upon his disciples, 'The world (i.e.,.., the Judean community), rests on three things, on the law, on Divine service, (In the Temple), and on Charity".
H. Graetz, History of the Jews, vol. One p.422

We will deal with the word cosmos in greater depth in the latter portion of this chapter. A third illustration of the distortion of the English word "world".....

Mathew 24:14

14 And this gospel of the kingdom shall be preached in all the *world* for a witness unto all nations; and then shall the end come. KJV

An essential appendage that the translators incorporated into Jesus' catastrophic narrative at the Mount of Olives cannot be ignored. The doctrine has fueled the modern Evangelical movement to incessantly propagate the Gospel into every crevice of the known and unknown world that we in which we live.

The prevailing understanding of its teaching is that the "end of the world" will coincide with the Gospel preached to "every creature" on the planet, and then the end will come. The sustained usage of the universal term "world" in Mathew 24 should expose the careless methods that were utilized by the translators. The Greek word in the case of Matthew 24:14 is oikoumene, which does not lend itself to be interpreted beyond a regional principality, as in this case, the Roman Empire. Its assumed universal usages in the New Testament are due to ignorance of the local, covenant nature of its narratives. For example:

Acts 24:5

5 For we have found this man (Paul) a pestilent fellow, and a mover of sedition among all the Jews *throughout the world* (oikoumene), and a ringleader of the sect of the Nazarenes:

Luke 2:1-3

1. And it came to pass in those days, that there went out a decree from   Cæsar Augustus, that the entire world (oikoumene) should be taxed.

2 (*And* this taxing was first made when Cyrenius was governor of Syria.)

3 And all went to be taxed, every one into his city. KJV

NT:3625 **oikoumene** (oy-kou-men'-ay); feminine participle present passive of NT:3611 (as noun, by implication of NT:1093); land, i.e. the (terrene part of the) globe; specifically, the Roman empire:

The Kosmos

The word kosmos has a philosophical bias inherently built within its etymology. It was influenced by the philosophy of Pythagoras, Plato, Aristotle, Philo, and Hellenistic Judaism, to name just a few. This philosophical view was superimposed over the ancient Hebraic narrative of Covenant Creation and has redefined the essential renderings of "heaven and earth."

"The case is different with the meanings "world/universe," which kosmos took on from the time of Plato as a central term of Greek philosophy.
According to Diogenes Laertius vi, i.1.24 and Plutarch *De Placitis Philosophorum ii.1, Pythagoras (6th cent. B.C.) was the first to designate the "total world" as kosmos because of the order inherent in it.* From the
time of the Ionic natural philosophy of the 6th cent. B.C., kosmos assumes an order or standard by which the things of the world are held together (Anaximander frag. 9). *Consequently the total world, when considered in spatial terms as world, is called kosmos in the sense of "universe" "inasmuch as in it all individual things and creatures, heaven and earth, gods and men, are brought into unity by a universal order" (Sasse 871; cf. Plato Grg..*
The Greek concept of kosmos was mediated to early

Christianity by Hellenistic Judaism, as is indicated esp. in the late and originally Greek writings of the LXX (cf. Wisdom 7:17; 9:3; 4 Macc 16:18, etc.) and in Philo.

*The Greek terminology **that has been adopted replaces the earlier Hebrew expression "heaven and earth" (Gen 1:1**), sometimes also "the totality" (Ps 8:7); however, it introduces a further development of the ideas of kosmos, one that gives a vocabulary to wisdom-apocalyptic dualism also within the realm of the terminology of the world and creation."*

The term cosmos—a patently loaded term— is very much infused with a conflation of suggestive inferences due to various etymological sources, a blend of Greek philosophy and Hellenistic/ Jewish concoctions that are foreign to the standard textural tradition modeled within the Torah. In spite of a wide range of possible applications for the word cosmos, we believe that the scribes of the New Testament utilized this word with full knowledge that its philological origins would be the final arbiter of the word's signification within the text.

It is known that ancient science and philosophical concepts integrated within the Greek language, and nowhere are this more apparent than with the word kosmos. The scribes of the first century utilized the language that best suited the publication of the gospel. Selecting the appropriate words to embody a proper translation of the Hebrew and Aramaic dictated from the lips of the Apostles proved to be a daunting task. To obscure the situation even further, add 2000 years of philosophical and social developments with translations meandering through Latin and German to produce our

Modern English Bibles. Sadly, our most cherished lexicons are tainted with scholarship nourished in secular universities where the philosophical tradition replicates their Western proclivities. In effect, the tail (New Testament Greek interpretation) is wagging the dog (The Old Testament narrative). If one would only master the simple admonition of maintaining covenantal parameters provided in the Torah, the balance of scripture would fall right into place.

The following excerpts from Gerhard Kittel's Theological Dictionary of the New Testament reveal the bias of its author regarding this word, especially his view of "the world" in universal terms. Nevertheless, he does record its nefarious pedigree when displacing "Heaven and Earth" by the universal interloper, *kosmos,* and this is telling. His lack of understanding of the imagery of "Heaven and Earth" apparently forced his hand to insert the Westernized notion of a cosmological signification.

Furthermore, we must also note that the rabbinical adaptation of this term served in the redefinition of the word OLAM (forever, perpetual, or everlasting). The notion of infinity was affixed to it in spite of its Hebraic implications of being concealed, out of mind, or beyond the horizon. As Kittel states: *a Hebrew word **like olam (forever) takes on a new special sense (cf. the rabbinic adoption of the word kosmos as a loan word)*** This statement only confirms our contention that Greek philosophy and its Hellenistic overtures not only redefined many Old Testament expressions but in effect have assisted in reinterpreting the New Testament through the lens of universalism. There is an abundance of textual evidence which contests the Hellenistic notion of infinity to the expression, "Olam" (forever). Here is one such text.

And thou — thou dost command the sons of Israel, and they bring unto thee pure beaten olive oil for the light, to cause the lamp to go up continually;

21 in the tent of meeting, at the outside of the vail, which [is] over the testimony, doth Aaron — his sons also — arrange it from evening till morning before Jehovah — a statute age-during to their generations, from the sons of Israel. YLT   (forever)

For further information regarding the encroachment of universalism into holy writ, please read the chapter entitled "All Things," as we go into greater detail into this topic.

Cosmos in Definition

Gerhard Kittel provides an array of usages for the word cosmos; here, we provide a sampling for your perusal:

> **<u>Non Biblical usage</u>**: *Order, what is well assembled or constructed, in right order.*
> 1. *The idea that there is an order of things that correspond **to the order of human law.***
> 2. *Beauty: since what is well ordered is also beautiful, kosmos may also denote "adornment; women, buildings, walls, cultic actions etc.*
> 3. *Spatial sense is undoubtedly **present in the fifth century B.C. questions of space and infinity** arise already in the natural philosophy of this period.*
> 4. *The idea that there is an order of things that*

5. *corresponds to* **the order of human law....***an imminent cosmic norm that upholds things together as the law does society. The world itself is viewed as an ordered society.*
6. *Plato uses it in the special sense, the merging of ideas in cosmic space and heavenly space so that heaven and the cosmos tend to be exchangeable terms.*
7. *Aristotle: the totality of things, the* **cosmos is in itself infinite.**

....

The following portion of Kettle's continued definition on kosmos is probably the most dominant source by which the New Testament scribes were typically influenced, although other influences cited in Kittel's article were sure to have been in vogue in the first century.

....

Kosmos in the LXX: The concept of kosmos in Judaism.

1. It makes the word kosmos a Biblical as well as ***a philosophical concept****. The LXX uses kosmos:*

a) For the host of heaven (Gen. 2:1), the stars
b) Adornment
c) The universe; thus ***substituting it*** *in such works as Wisdom and Maccabees* ***for the older term "heaven and earth."***

*2. Since cosmos for universe becomes common only in the later Greek works, it is obviously adopted by Hellenistic Judaism from contemporary usage and **bears some imprint of philosophical teaching.***

*3. Under the influence of the use of the word kosmos, a Hebrew word **like olam (forever) takes on a new special sense (cf. the rabbinic adoption of the word kosmos as a loan word)***

4. The Greek idea of humanity as a microcosm also finds its way into rabbinical thinking.

Kosmos in the New Testament

*1. "Jesus frequently articulated "Heaven and Earth" for the cosmos... **As universe, cosmos is synonymous with the old testament "Heaven and Earth."***

2. Kosmos as world, the universe the sum of all created being.

*a. **As universe, kosmos is synonymous with O.T. heaven and earth.***

3. Kosmos as world : the abode of humanity, the theater of history, the inhabited world, the Earth.

4. Kosmos as world, Humanity, fallen creation and the setting of the salvation of history.

*"The implication is that the human world falls victim to divine judgment because it is the evil world. Judaism develops this thought to some extent, especially in apocalyptic which shows some influence of Persian dualism. **Yet Hellenistic Judaism, which inherits***

Hellenistic joy in the world, maintains a more optimistic view on the basis of the fact that the cosmos is God's creation."

....

As with most scholars, Kittel disregarded the prospect of a "covenant world" when analyzing these narratives and persisted in forcing the issue of kosmos in Platonic terms. Note the scriptural illustrations he uses in the following excerpts of his definition.

Kittel proposes:

a. The whole cosmos (humanity) is thus guilty before God. Rom.3:19 and under his judgment Rom.3:6 and condemnation. Cor. 11:32
It was the rulers of the kosmos who crucified the Lord of glory. 1Cor. 2:8

b. For God was in Christ reconciling the kosmos
unto himself. Cor.2:19

c. Christ's history is true human history, but the
whole universe has a part of it. Rom. 8:22, Col.
8:16

In true covenantal context:
- The New Testament ascribes guilt to the cosmos (the Jews) because they were **under the Law** of covenant relationship through Moses.
- Israel (kosmos) was **under judgment** because of its disobedience. Ascribing guilt to the unwashed masses of humanity is a grievous error that most scholars make.

The world (cosmos) of Aristotle did not crucify the Lord of glory; the Jews were responsible for his death.

- Christ did not reconcile the world (kosmos) of Philo to Himself; he came to and died for the people of Israel.
- The true light which lights every man comes into the covenant world, not into the world (kosmos) of Pythagoras.
- The saints do not judge the world (kosmos) of Hellenism; they adjudicate Biblical Law among themselves as they order their lives before the Lord.
- The population of this world (kosmos) does not groan with anticipation for the manifestation of the sons of God; they couldn't care less. The expectation of redemption was exclusively a kingdom expectation.

....

Kittle continues:

a. The whole cosmos (humanity) is thus guilty before God. Rom.3:19 and under his judgment Rom.3:6 and condemnation. Cor. 11:32
It was the rulers of the kosmos who crucified the Lord of glory. 1Cor. 2:8
b. For God was in Christ reconciling the kosmos unto himself. Cor.2:19
c. Christ's history is true human history but the whole universe has a part of it. Rom. 8:22, Col.8:16"

....

We would be greatly negligent not to concede that the introduction of the Greek language fostered a legitimate impact on the cultural views of those of the first century. Western cultural awareness does find a way to express some essential nuances to the narrative that the Hebrew may have found complicated in expressing in its idiom. Even the usage of the word kosmos does indeed illustrate the world of Rome. Such inferences to an external unsaved world also acknowledged by this author; references to a cosmic creation are also in order in other instances. The great objection that we do have is not with the Greek language per se; it is with the misguided inferences and interpretations generated by scholars through the imposition of extra-biblical philosophies into the sacred text. Thus, these scholars have reinvented the New Testament in their image. This re-creation of the Biblical narrative has caused a rupture in the essentially consonant relationship between Genesis and Revelation, especially as about their kindred prophetic objectives. The beginning does not resemble the end, although its imagery unmistakably generates it by its correlating poetry and symbolism. The impossible verdict of our betters has implied that the end of the prophetic writ (Revelation) is a deviation from its beginning, thus relegating (Genesis) to an irrelevant discharge of Science and History.

There are three that bear witness in the earth
1 John 5:8

8 And there are three that bear witness in earth, the Spirit, and the water, and the blood: and these three agree in one. KJV

The language of the preceding text should persuade us to pause and to reflect again upon the usage of the word *earth*. The identification of the elements of blood, water, and spirit bring proper contextual order to the passage. These elements (blood, water, and spirit) used in conjunction with covenantal overtones while symbolically portraying the work of Christ as imputed unto his people. In assessing various parts of the biblical record, we find that the Apostle John draws on a previously established pattern to make an important statement regarding the redeeming aspects of the New Testament rebirth. Jesus initiated this pattern when he spoke to Nicodemus (Acts 3:5) and told that he was required to be born again "of the *water and the spirit*" to gain admission into the Kingdom of God.

John 3:5

5 Jesus answered, Verily, verily, I say unto thee, Except a man be born of water and the Spirit, he can not enter into the kingdom of God. KJV

Jesus never concretely specified how one might access the kingdom of God through "the water and the spirit," but we do hear the preaching of Peter and the Apostles as they gave specific commands to all who desired to embrace their Messiah in that new birth experience of the blood, water, and spirit.

Acts 2:38

38 Then Peter said unto them, Repent, and be baptized every one of you in the name of Jesus Christ for the remission of sins, and ye shall receive the gift of the Holy Ghost. KJV

21 Now he which stablisheth us with you in Christ, and hath *anointed us*, *is* God;

22 Who hath also *sealed us, and given the earnest of the Spirit in our hearts*. KJV

Hebrews 13:12

12 Wherefore Jesus also, that he might *sanctify the people with his own blood,* suffered without the gate. KJV

John 19:34

34 But one of the soldiers with a spear pierced his side, and forthwith came there out *blood and water*. KJV

Thus, the blood, the water, and the spirit are not just theoretical components of salvation. The transforming power and renewal apprehended in the "earth," or the earthly constituency serves as a witness to all that the kingdom of God is indeed among men. Mere religion cannot accomplish this; it can only be attained through the supernatural embodiment of the death, burial, and resurrection by those who believe.

The Witnesses against Heaven and Earth

The imagery of heaven and earth also functions as a witness adjudicating the guilt of its people for the time of wrath. The principle of the first mention for this standard directs us to Deuteronomy 17:6-7. Under the Mosaic code there must be at least two or three witnesses to furnish corroborating evidence as concerning a capital crime. As we all know, the accusers of Christ were unable to achieve that basic requirement for his execution. This standard enacted at the codification of the Mosaic covenant as a warning of the dire consequences of its breach.

The development of this imagery persists in the vision of the two olive trees in Zechariah 4:3. The prophet asked the angel to identify the olive trees to the left and right side of the golden lampstand, i .e.the sons of oil. The lampstand is considered by many to be a representation of the Tree of Life, as illustrated in the pages of Genesis and Revelation. Its imagery is also notably employed in the first chapter of Revelation as Jesus portrayed amid seven Churches. The Tree of Life depicted as the source of healing for the nations, the primary function of the Church in this life. Furthermore, the olive tree consistently portrayed as spiritual Israel, the anointed, whiles the Fig Tree and its fruit as entities of naughtiness and cursing. The Angel responded to the prophet's query, 'these [are] ***the two sons of the oil***, who are standing by the Lord of the whole earth.' YLT

Admittedly, if we were to select two personages from the narrative of Zachariah chapters three and four, it would be Zerubbabel and Joshua the high priest. They were the heads of government and spiritual life in Jerusalem at that time. That would be an educated assumption, but it does not definitively settle the issue of these two witnesses. The logical development of this principle culminates in the book of Revelation 11:3-4. The eternal guessing game as to the identity of these witnesses can now be put to rest through the simple relationship of its first mention and its sustained use in the prophetic record. The imagery of the two witnesses in Revelation 11 calls down the curses of a breached covenant as prescribed by Deuteronomy. The fire commanded by the two witnesses originates from the Lord, which is a product of the preaching of the Church during the tribulation. The Church personified in this activity through the imagery of these two witnesses. The Greek word for the word witness is martus or martyr. It is the same word as is used in Revelation 11:3- 4)

Acts 1:8

8 But ye shall receive power, after that the Holy
Ghost is come upon you: and ye shall be (martyrs)
witnesses unto me both in Jerusalem, and in all Judæa,
and Samaria, and unto the uttermost part of the earth.

There are no personalities of mention in the entire text of Revelation that one could select for this role portrayed in Revelation 11. The prophetic type of judgment is found in Moses as he brings each of the ten plagues upon Egypt. Revelation 11:8 metaphorically ascribes the name of Sodom and Egypt to the place where our Lord was born. By this evidence; we can safely conclude that the locality and recipient of the plagues in Revelation 11 was Jerusalem, its temple and the disobedient of that age

Deuteronomy 17:6-7

6 At the mouth of two witnesses, or three witnesses,
shall he that is worthy of death be put to death; *but* at

the mouth of one witness, he shall not be put to death.

7 The hands of the witnesses shall be first upon him to put him to death, and afterward, the hands of all the people. So thou shalt put the evil away from among you. KJV

Zechariah 4:2-5

2 And said unto me, What seest thou? And I said, I have looked, and behold a candlestick all *of* gold, with a bowl upon the top of it, and his seven lamps thereon, and seven pipes to the seven lamps, which *are* upon the top thereof:

3 And two olive trees by it, one upon the right *side* of the bowl, and the other upon the left *side* thereof.

4 So I answered and spake to the angel that talked with me, saying, What *are* these, my lord?

5 Then the angel that talked with me answered and said unto me, Knowest thou not what these be? And I said, No, my lord.

Zechariah 4:11-14

11 And I answer and say unto him, 'What [are] these two olive-trees, on the right of the candlestick, and on its left?'

12 And I answer a second time, and say unto him, 'What [are] the two branches of the olive trees that, by means of the two golden pipes, are emptying out of themselves the oil?'

13 And he speaketh unto me, saying, 'Hast thou not known what these [are]?' And I say, 'No, my lord.'

14 And he saith, 'These [are] *the two sons of the oil*, who are standing by the Lord of the whole earth.' YLT

Revelation 11:3-4

3 And I will give *power* unto my two (martyrs) witnesses, and they shall prophesy a thousand two hundred *and* threescore days, clothed in sackcloth.

4 These are the two olive trees, and the two candlesticks standing before the God of the earth.

The following passage exhibits this Hebraic prose as these dual expressions; "words in their ears," and "call heaven and earth" reiterate the command to communicate as a witness against itself and its leadership.

Deuteronomy 31:28-29

28 Gather unto me all *the elders of your tribes, and your officers*, that I may speak these **words in their ears**, and **call_heaven and earth** *to record against them.*

29 For I know that after my death ye will utterly corrupt *yourselves*, and turn aside from the way which I have commanded you; and evil will befall you in the latter days; because ye will do evil in the sight of the Lord, to provoke him to anger through the work of your hands. KJV

Deuteronomy 4:26

26 I call heaven and earth to witness against you this day, that ye shall soon utterly perish from off the land whereunto ye go over Jordan to possess it; ye shall not prolong *your* days upon it, but shall utterly be destroyed KJV

Hebrew parallelism both contrasts and harmonizes the subject by addressing the earth and its mountains in verse two while poetically integrating "my people" and "Israel" in symbolic unison.

Micah 6:2-3

2 Hear ye, O mountains, the Lord's controversy, and ye strong foundations of the earth: for the Lord hath a controversy with his people, and he will plead with Israel.

3 O my people, what have I done unto thee? and wherein have I wearied thee? testify against me. KJV

The Heavens and the Earth Standing in and out of the Water

The absurdity of taking verse five of the following text in its literal form is quite telling because the proponents of such future universal destruction ignore the absolute impracticality of their hypothesis. A question that Bible students should ask themselves: How did the heavens and the earth stand in and out of the water? The answer is terrifyingly simple. They (Heaven and Earth) were in the Ark; in the water and out of the water. There are two possible ways to view this statement:

1. As a passenger of any boat, we are technically in the water with the boat and also out of the water, thereby evading its wetness.

2. Those who perished and those who were delivered were covenant people, thus we have those who perished in the water and those who survived out of the water by being in the Ark.

2 Peter 3:5

5 But in taking this view they put out of their minds the memory that in the old days there was a heaven, and an earth lifted out of the water and circled by water, by the word of God;

The Bible in Basic English

One must develop cognitive dissonance to ignore such a blatant departure from the realm of common sense. Peter used the flood as a type to foreshadow the day of the Lord. He utilized its destruction as a proof text for his statements concerning the judgment of the heaven and earth of his era; (this time to be dissolved by fire verse 12). But again, we have been willingly ignorant as we evaded the imagery of "the heavens being on fire." Unconsciously we have decided to overlook the impossibility of these statements to accommodate the urging of a universal cataclysm prescribed by our particular denominations.

2 Peter 3:5-7

5 For this they willingly are ignorant of, that by the word of God the heavens were of old, and the earth standing out of the water and in the water:

6 Whereby the world that then was, being overflowed with water, perished:

7 But the heavens and the earth, which are now, by the same word, are kept in store, reserved unto fire against the Day of Judgment and perdition of ungodly men.

The Heavens pass away...The Earth burnt up

Perhaps the most striking imagery that has pierced our collective consciousness is found in 2 Peter 3:10-13. Its highly symbolic portrayal of covenantal transitioning takes on a literal three - dimensional expectation of the total annihilation of our universe. By ignoring its broad overview of prophetic patterns, Christian teachers have, in effect, created their rigid narrative that persists within an air-tight vacuum. We say in a vacuum because the conclusions of those who endorse these notions bear little resemblance to the Ancient Hebraic sentiments found in the Old Testament text. The book of Revelation is another profound example of the same issue. The symbolism in Revelation is merely the summation of the prophetic record that precedes it, and yet great swaths of the text have been reinvented in a modern format for the consumption of greater Churchianity; as a result, we've all been "left behind?!"

The "Day of the Lord" is not speaking of a chronological day but a prophetic day. As we continue our study in this volume, we will discuss the seven days of Genesis One in terms of their prophetic properties. Yes, the expression "day of the Lord," as expressed throughout the sacred text is rooted in those early passages of Genesis. Therefore, the imagery of 2 Peter 3:10 indelibly integrated into that same ancient Hebraic tradition. Thus, the balance of the text must follow suit by this primary affirmation. The phrase "thief in the night" also maintains its prophetic pedigree as it yoked with its primary prophetic designation, "the day of the Lord," and its mention in the Mount Olivet discourse (Matt. 24:43). The intent of both phrases is in lockstep as they lay the foundation for the allegorical narrative that follows.

What needs to be acknowledged is the simplicity of the linguistic imagery of fire in conjunction with the age-old expressions such as "the fire of his vengeance" and that "God is a consuming fire." Historically, these phrases were never a product of literalization, but we quickly disregard the significance of this imagery with the destruction of the heavens by fire. These metaphoric gestures convey the vengeance and judgment of God. The continued expectation of a new *physical* heaven and earth where "righteousness dwells" thrusts the entire narrative into the sphere of the bizarre. When one should inquire into such a nebulous account, we, inadvertently, enter into the realm of conjecture. A kind of Twilight Zone of diversity develops where one view is as good as another so long as we all agree that we maintain the devastation and restoration of the material cosmos…

2 Peter 3:10-13

10 But the day of the Lord will come as a thief in the night; in the which the heavens shall pass away with a great noise and the elements shall melt with fervent

heat, the earth also and the works that are therein shall be burned up.

11 *Seeing* then *that* all these things shall be dissolved, what manner *of persons* ought ye to be in *all* holy conversation and godliness,

12 Looking for and hasting unto the coming of the day of God, wherein the heavens being on fire shall be dissolved, and the elements shall melt with fervent heat?

13 Nevertheless we, according to his promise, look for new heavens and a new earth, wherein dwelleth righteousness.

We have not accorded the subject of "heaven and earth" its due in this short essay, but we hope that by introducing this important subject early in this volume that it would function as an essential primer for related imagery to follow.

Chapter Two
In the Beginning God Bara

Genesis 1:1-2

1:1 In the beginning God *created* the Heaven and the *earth*.

2 And the earth was without form, and void; and darkness was upon the face of the deep. And the Spirit of God moved upon the face of the waters. KJV

Genesis 1:1-2

1. In the summit Elohiym *fattened the sky and the land*

2. and the land had existed in confusion and was unfulfilled and darkness was upon the face of the deep sea and the wind of Elohim was much fluttering upon the face of the water.

Jeff Benner, Mechanical Translation of the Book of Genesis, p.15 2007

Creation in Filling and Forming

A word of great consequence within the first verse of the Bible is the word *created (bara)*. Our modern rendering of the word bara has inadvertently altered its original Hebraic meaning to construct matter out of nothing. The Hebrews never understood our Westernized concept of constructing matter out of nothing. Such an abstract concept does not undergird any biblical text in existence. The true prophetic disclosure of the creative process of "bara" the Bible illustrates in separation, nurturing, and development through the empowerment of the word of God. The Vines Hebrew Dictionary interjects a Western concept regarding the word"bara" That approach is not evident in any Biblical text in existence. On the other hand, the word "bara" reveals the true intent of creation as one of separation, nurturing, and development through the empowerment of the word of God.

The Vines Hebrew dictionary interjects a western cosmological interpretation to the word "bara" *only when about Genesis One.* It tells us that *all other* usages to the word "bara" have nothing to do with someone or something coming into existence from nothingness. It is interesting to note that Vine's does not give the reasoning for such a claim, and it might be aptly advanced that this demonstrates a prime example of textual bias practiced by noted lexicons. Certainly, we would all do well to beware of such heedless inclinations while inquiring into such "enlightened" volumes.

Vines Expository Dictionary:

bara' OT:1254 "to create, make." This verb is of profound theological significance since it has only God as its subject. Only God can "create" in a sense implied by bara'. The verb expresses *__creation out of nothing__*, an idea is seen clearly in passages having to do with creation on a **cosmic** scale: "In the beginning, God created the heaven and the earth" Genesis 1:1; cf. Genesis 2:3; Isaiah 40:26; 42:5. *__All other verbs for "creating"__ allow a much broader range of meaning; they have both divine and human subjects and are used in contexts where bringing something or someone into existence is not the issue.* **Vine Expository Dictionary of Biblical Words, Nelson Publishers**

"furthermore, the word bara, to create, does not, according to Hebrew, signify the original production of the material or substance of that which is brought into being.

*This is **only the notion of some modern writers**. In Genesis 1:21 the word is applied to the bringing forth of creatures which are expressly said to have been produced <u>from the waters</u> , and in verse 27 it is used of man who was formed in part of <u>the dust of the ground...</u> We may, therefore, properly understand it, in Genesis 1:1 as denoting the forming or construction out of pre-existing material....* Milton Terry *Biblical Hermeneutics second edition p549 (1883)*

"Essentially, the proper Hebraic perception of this word denotes to fill, cut, enrich, or to fatten. The word create always implies that the subject in question necessitates development, formation, or rehabilitation. In Paleo Hebrew, the word bara (create) is related to the word son, or bar, which is depicted as a floor plan for a tent or house followed with a man's head and is rendered "house or family of heads." **Benner**

The Hebrews took this to mean a cluster of seeds at the top of the stalk called "heads." Livestock fed on these heads of grain. Thus, the ancients understood the text through the idioms of their language. Gesenius writes that it is a son, and is from the idea of begetting. The begetting of sons or generations of sons is crucial to the narrative of Genesis chapters 1 and 2.

Genesis 2:4

4 These [are] births of the heavens and of the earth in their being prepared, in the day of Jehovah God's making earth and heavens; YLT

Strong's: bar #1249, means chosen, beloved, clean, and separated.

Bar#1250, means grain cleansed from chaff, (this should sound very familiar.)

Soap was made from the ashes of the burned stalks to make potash for soap. The word for soap doubles the head on the diagram. This signifies to clean or defined as soap.*   ***Benner ב ר ר.**

Grain was cleaned by sifting before consumption. The theme of separation in covenant relationship seems built into the language of creation." This theme of sifting or separation dominates the first six days of Genesis One; light from darkness, waters from the waters, and the waters from dry land. This process is developed in the chapter entitled, "The wisdom of Creation."

*<u>OT:1254</u> † **verb be fat** (Arabic *be free of a thing, sound, healthy*;

Bara (ברא) Depicted as the floor plan for a tent or house, a man's head, and the head of a bull. Gesenius affirms that it means to eat, to feed, to grow fat, so-called from cutting food, to fatten, to be well fed.

Another related word in this family of expressions is Beriyth or covenant. The basic aspects of its root relationships with Bara, Bar, and Barr constitute the components of Beriyth and visa versa. These words generate a composite picture of the true narrative of

Genesis One. The false narrative concocted by a literal, universal motif falls flat when we deliberate the ancient value of these words.

Beriyth has been understood to mean, "To cut the meat," a ceremonial tradition among the ancients in the Near and Middle East. After slaughtering the animals of the covenant, the parties then walked through the midst of the carcasses to underscore the penalty of death to the defaulting party. Most agreements in the biblical record secured through a personal agreement, and, a large feast or banquet would ensue.

Covenant, Beriyth OT:1285

L. Kohler claims the word was related to the root ברה, which has to do with the food and eating involved in the covenant meal (JSS 1: 4-7). The root is nowhere used as a verb in the OT nor is any other derivative of this root used, but the action involving covenant-making employs the idiom **"to cut a covenant"** (Gen 15:18; etc.), that is, making a bloody sacrifice as part of the covenant ritual, Kohler **then would have the animal eaten in the covenant meal**.

(from Theological Wordbook of the Old Testament. Copyright © 1980 by The Moody Bible Institute of Chicago. All rights reserved. Used by permission.)

According to Strong's, Beriyth is indeed organically tied to the word Bara. The implications of this are mind-boggling when we consider that within the etymology of the word Beriyth, the cutting (alluded to it by most lexicons) has "the same sense of cutting [like OT 1254] (Bara)

OT:1285 Covenant **beriyth** (ber-eeth'); from OT:1262 **(in the sense of cutting [like** ; a compact (because made by passing between pieces of flesh): - confederacy, [con-] feder [-ate], covenant, league.

(Biblesoft's New Exhaustive Strong's Numbers and Concordance with Expanded Greek-Hebrew Dictionary. Copyright © 1994, 2003, 2006 Biblesoft, Inc. and International Bible Translators, Inc.)

Strong's concordance agrees with the Paleo Hebrew in stating the following:

OT:1254 Create; Bara a primitive root; (absolutely) to create; (qualified) to cut down (a wood), select, *feed (as formative processes):* -choose, create (creator), cut down, dispatch, do, *make (fat).*

(Biblesoft's New Exhaustive Strong's Numbers and Concordance with Expanded Greek-Hebrew Dictionary

Gesenius also agrees:
1254 Create; to eat, to feed, to grow fat so-called from cutting food.

Gesenius Hebrew Chaldee Lexicon to the Old Testament p.139

If what these lexicons say is correct, then it begs the question: what is being filled, cleansed, and fattened, is it livestock? No, I dare say that these definitions concur within the balance of the Biblical narrative, its process of new birth as sons, its systematic progression of sanctification, and the general formation of covenant believers in nourishing and establishing them according to a blood covenant.

The misguided rendering of the word Bara in Genesis One invites a need for the insertion of a more appropriate English word in substitution for the word "created." As we have previously noted, our perception of the word "created" denotes something made out of nothing; this is due to a prevailing addiction to the tradition of ancient Western philosophy and its far-reaching religious propaganda. If the word Bara rendered "to create something out of nothing," we would not have a leg to stand on regarding the issues raised in the study of covenant creation. The entire issue of a universal cosmic creation rises and falls upon the interpretation of that one word. The nature of that activity (creation) must also lend itself to the balance of the sacred text as it further develops; otherwise, it will not thrive in its intended purpose and ultimately ceases to function as a viable component of the overall Biblical narrative. In other words, Genesis One was not written to linger within the confinement of ancient history and the fuzzy scientific speculations of historical creationism. In our estimation, the patterns of Genesis One continue to function and thrive throughout scripture in a holistic prophetic form — a perpetuating covenantal dynamic— and not as an isolated cosmological event.

"The scripture emphasize the action of God as creator. There are many facets to the subject of creation. But one thing is clear: God has brought into existence all that is. He creates, forms, makes what he wants for the purposes he has in mind. Creation not only involves matter and persons but also the transformation of a rebel into a disciple and a sinner into a consecrated Christian (2 Cor. 5:17) Creation is past and present. But there is also a future dimension of creation. This future aspect gives meaning and unity to scripture and history."
Interpreting the Bible; Mickelsen p.86

The word <u>formed</u> is closely associated with the word create; they are essentially viewed synonymously in most cases. Both words function the same way very much.

Both words indicate more of the process of covenant development as opposed to an event in ancient history. The Hebrew word Yatzar means to form or fashion. It is used as a potter that forms a vessel out of clay (Jer. 18: 4,6) ....the verb "form" used as a synonym for the word "create"...

"To understand better the significance of Gods' activity of forming or fashioning in Genesis 2 one should see how the expression is used of God in other contexts. The theme that God formed Israel as a people is a prominent one. God formed Israel from the womb (Isaiah 44: 1-2, 24) ..."Thus saith Jehovah, the holy one of Israel even the one forming him ...(Isaiah 45:11).. but now Jehovah you are our father and we are the clay, and you are the one forming us. And all of us are the works of your hand. (Isaiah 64:8) The word formed in the proceeding two references is Qual, active participle. The active participle in Hebrew indicates a person or thing conceived as being in the continual uninterrupted exercise of an activity. This indicates that God did not bring Israel into existence as a nation by one instantaneous act. Rather in Isaiah's day he was still fashioning the nation even though more than a millennium had passed since he had first called Abraham to be the father of a great multitude... The word form is used as a parallel expression for the word make in Isaiah 27:11 and for the word create in Isaiah 43:1" **Interpreting the Bible,1963 Mickelsen p. 310**

Taking what Mickelsen states on the meaning and Biblical treatment of the words *create, form,* and *make* only substantiates our contention that the general assumption of the usage of the word *create* (as in making "something out of nothing") does not hold much water. If these words are so closely identified to one another contextually, then the opening statement of Holy Writ in Genesis1:1 could have possibly stated: "In the beginning, God *formed* the heaven and the earth," or "In the beginning, God *made* the heaven and the earth."

If the usage of the word *formed* in Genesis 2:7 infers Mickelson's "continual, uninterrupted exercise of an activity," the corporate implication of the word Adam in this text (as acknowledged by Gesenius) would agree with Mickelson's view of Israel's covenantal development throughout history. Mickelson's view helps to transform a perceived singular event in history to one that is continually in the throes of maturation.

The confusion over the word "create" has even further mystified us with its contrived assertions. In the following passage, one is led to assume that God is the source of all evil in the universe. One can only come to that conclusion if we infer the assumptions of the cosmological motif of a literal universal creation. The passage is merely reiterating the theme of God's redemption in man as He transforms the hearts of men through a covenant relationship. The word *form* in this scripture means to squeeze into shape or to mold. Hebraic poetry reiterates this sentiment by utilizing the word *bara*, or *create* interchangeably with comparative synoptic relationships to reemphasize its message of redemption. God rehabilitates evil (the dysfunctional), makes peace, and forms man according to his sovereign will.

Isaiah 45:7-8

7 I *form* the light,

and *create* (enrich or rehabilitate) darkness:

I *make* peace,

and **create** (enrich or rehabilitate) **evil:**

I the Lord do all these things.

8 Drop down, ye heavens, from above,

and let the skies **pour down righteousness**:

let the earth open, and *let them bring forth salvation*,

and let righteousness spring up together;

I the Lord have **created)** (enriched) it.

Or

Isaiah 45:7

Forming light and filling the darkness, making wholeness and filling dysfunction I am Yahweh doing all of these.

New and Old Testament Correlations of the Word Creation

The New Testament usage of the word creation or creature also reflects the same usage for the word creation in the Old Testament. The underlying usage and sentiment of these expressions agree contextually in both the New and Old Testaments, especially with covenant creation. As in all instances, the text should be the sole arbiter for

108

determining word usage in a passage. Regrettably, the predisposed notions of fixed oral traditions have advanced its theological agenda, all with universal acclaim. Thus, it is nigh impossible to arrive at a Biblically reasoned conclusion with that brand of careless methodology.

The English word **creation or creature** is used interchangeably in the Greek. They are not two different Greek words. Unfortunately, the English translations do not divulge its common origin. The Septuagint properly applied the Greek word create, (ktizoo N.T.2936) as to create in Genesis 1:1. We believe that these ancient Greek scribes understood that the words "bara" and "ktizoo" are used interchangeably and that they utilized them so many times throughout the Old Testament. The New Testament function of this word does not conform to the prevailing cosmological view of the word "create" in the following passages:

NT:2936 ktizoo:

Septuagint chiefly for bara; properly, **to make habitable,** to people, a place, region, island

(from Thayer's Greek Lexicon, Electronic Database. Copyright © 2000, 2003 by Biblesoft, Inc. All rights reserved.)

Galatians 6:15

15 For in Christ Jesus neither circumcision availeth anything, nor uncircumcision, but a new **creature** (creation).

2 Corinthians 5:17

17 Therefore if any man be in Christ, he is a new **creature** (creation): old things are passed away; behold, all things are become new…

 Romans 8:22-23
22 For we know that the whole **creation** groaneth and travaileth in pain together until now.

Ephesians 4:24

24 And that ye put on the new man, which after God is **created** in righteousness and true holiness.

Ephesians 2:10

10 For we are his workmanship, _created_ in Christ Jesus unto good works, which God hath before ordained that we should walk in them.

Old Testament Function

David desired regeneration of the heart and the spirit after his horrific behavior with Bathsheba. The degenerate state of David did not necessitate the "creation" of a new _physical_ heart. David needed a revival of what he already possessed. Restoration and rehabilitation is the focal point of the following Psalm. David desired the enrichment and reinstatement of _bara_ to fatten and to nurture his heart.

Psalms 51:10

10 Create in me a clean heart, O God; and renew a right spirit within me.

In the following scripture, the English word create is discarded for the correct intended expression of the word bara. Its meaning is apparent as it reveals its proper rudimentary underpinnings.

1 Samuel 2:29

29 Wherefore kick ye at my sacrifice and at mine offering, which I have commanded in my habitation; and honourest thy sons above me, **to make yourselves fat (bara)** with the chiefest of all the offerings of Israel my people? KJV

The word "bara" (created) in the following passage predicts the creation of a future generation that will praise the Lord. How will this be accomplished in light of our Western view of the word create? In essence, this passage concurs with the New Testament concerning the continuance of the covenant birthings of heaven and earth.

Psalms 102:18

8 Let this be written for a future generation, that a people not yet **created** may praise the Lord NIV

Psalm 104 is yet another departure from the motif of an ancient historical creation by its usage of the present tense. The cycle of de-creation (vs. 29) and

re-creation (fattening) is well represented here with the on again off again covenant relationship between God and man.

Psalms 104:29-30
29 You hide Your face, they are troubled;

You take away their breath, they die and return to their dust.
30 You send forth Your Spirit, they are **created (fattened)**; And You **renew (repair)** the face of the earth.

God Recreates a New Heaven and a New Earth

Re-creation verbiage is patterned after the language of Genesis One as it replicates its imagery through the promises of reconciliation and restoration. Note the references in the following passage to beasts of the field, the fowls of heaven, and the creeping things of the ground. The reintroduction of this theme can only point to a re-creation. The passage states that God would betroth and make a new covenant with these creatures. This genre of prophetic identification designates them as God's people. Examples of this kind of imagery found throughout the sacred text. It amounts to a reenactment of the covenant relationships evidenced in Genesis One and Two.

Hosea 2:18-21

18 And in that day will **I make a covenant for them** with **the beasts of the field, and with the fowls of heaven, and with the creeping things of the ground:** and I will break the bow and the sword and the battle out of the earth, and will make them to lie down safely.

19 And I will betroth thee unto me for ever; yea, I will betroth thee unto me in righteousness, and in judgment, and in loving kindness, and in mercies.

20 I will even betroth thee unto me in faithfulness: and thou shalt know the Lord.

In Isaiah 65:17-18, the prophet stated that the Lord would do some more creating. The Old Heavens and the Old Earth fell out of favor with God, and that necessitated the institution of a new order. It would require a new covenant requiring a New Testament. The prophetic relationship between the New Heavens, New Earth, and New Jerusalem are forged together and function interchangeably in Old and New Testament writings. Many Bible teachers teach that these terms are unrelated as Biblical synonyms, although they readily admit the concepts are associated with the scriptural narrative. Biblical evidence does not support their contradictory positions. For example, Isaiah 65:17-18 and Revelation 21:1-2 enjoins the concepts beautifully. *Question:* is God creating a new heaven and a new earth in Isaiah 65, or is he creating a New Jerusalem? The answer to this question is that these terms are symbolically interchangeable. In the true tradition of Hebrew poetry, the primary subject matter enshrined through its recurring usage.

Isaiah 65:17-18

17 For, behold, *I create* new *heavens* and a new *earth*: and the former (heaven and earth) shall not be remembered, nor come into mind.

18 But be ye glad and rejoice for ever in that which *I create*: for, behold, *I create Jerusalem a rejoicing, and her people a joy*. KJV

Revelation 21 repeats the same pattern as Isaiah 65 as it establishes the intent of its prophetic objective.

Revelation 21:1-2

And I saw a **new heaven and a new earth**: for the first heaven and the first earth (old heaven and earth) were passed away; and there was no more sea.

2 And I John saw the holy city, **New Jerusalem**, coming down from God out of heaven, prepared as a bride adorned for her husband KJV

De-creation

A classic misrepresentation of dire predictions of the destruction of old heavens and the old earth, according to the Apostle Peter, is legendary. The following passage is a poster child for what we term comic book theology where the undermining of true and inspired prophetic teaching becomes a caricature of itself. As a result, it has propelled Christianity along a wild goose chase going nowhere. Entire denominations are guilty of gross negligence because they completely ignore the Old Testament language of covenant attributed to heaven and earth that precedes salvation in the New Testament. The current promotion of the phrase, "the heavens being on fire," is patently absurd. The embracing of such a view would imply that inanimate objects are judged and destroyed, but there is simply no stated purpose for such a judgment. There is absolutely no hermeneutical pattern to support such a view.

12 Looking for and hasting unto the coming of the day of God, wherein the heavens being on fire shall be dissolved, and the elements shall melt with fervent heat?

13 Nevertheless, we, according to his promise, look for *new heavens and a new earth,* wherein dwelleth righteousness. KJV

The second verse of the Bible illustrates a picture of total devastation as contrasted by the depiction of functional heavens and earth in verse one. The recurrence of this theme evidenced throughout the sacred text. We usually find it associated with scriptures illustrating covenant people in a state of apostasy. The words void, empty, waste, dust, dung, darkness, waste, and desolate are just a few of the expressions used to communicate the profound deterioration of a covenant relationship with God.

Genesis 1:2

2 And the earth was without form, and void; and darkness was upon the face of the deep. And the Spirit of God moved upon the face of the waters.

One of the most amazing scriptures that we have discovered to support our position located in Jeremiah 4:22-23. The prophet bemoans the abysmal condition of his people, particularly given the dreadful judgment they were about to experience. If we consider Hebrew parallelism and its emphasis upon the repetition of subject matter, then verses 22 and 23 are expressing the same things about Israel. The repetitive verbiage of Genesis One is not inconsequential here but is instead a deliberate reference to its primary covenant usage (first mention). The reference would be of little merit if Genesis 1:2 merely alluded to an ancient cosmic event. The subject here is people, children, they, and earth. All of these expressions refer to one group of people.

Jeremiah 4:22-23

22. For my **people is foolish**,

they have **not known me**;

they are **sottish children**,

and they **have none understanding**:

they are **wise to do evil,**

but to do good **they have no knowledge.**

23 I beheld **the earth,**

and, lo, it was **without form,**

 and; **void** and the heavens,

 and **they had no light.**

A hundred and fifty years after the preaching of Jonah, the prophet Nahum pronounced judgment upon the people of Nineveh. The imagery of Genesis One was used to communicate God's displeasure with them. This manner of phraseology, we term "decreation." Its imagery is to illustrate a return to the pre-covenant status of Genesis 1:2.

 Nahum 2:10

10 She is **empty,**

 and **void,**

 and **waste:**

 and the **heart melteth,**
 and the **knees smite together,**

 and much **pain is in all loins,**

and the faces of them **all gather blackness**.

This is another good illustration:

Zephaniah 1:14-15

14 The great day of the Lord is near, it is near, and hasteth greatly, even the voice of the day of the Lord: the mighty man shall cry there bitterly.

15 That day is
   a day of **wrath,**
    a day of **trouble**
    and **distress,**
     a day of **wasetness**
     and **desolation,**
      a day **of darkness**
      and **gloominess,**
      a day **of clouds**
      and **thick darkness,**

In Isaiah 24, the prophet portrayed Israel in its dreadful condition. Isaiah did so by utilizing similar expressions found in Genesis 1:2. Note the way the passage refers to Israel as "the earth" as the context frames its covenantal implications. Also, the curious mention of the earth *mourning* as it depicts the heart-wrenching drama of a nation appraising its woeful state. If our assessment is incorrect, the fulfillment of these dreadful events would have a notation in the historical record, but they are not. Verse 1 declares that the earth is empty, waste, and turned upside down. The passage was written as a factual statement, and according to its account, the events occurred during the time of Isaiah.

Isaiah 24:1-2

24:1 Behold, the Lord maketh the earth empty, and maketh it waste, and turneth it upside down, and scattereth abroad the inhabitants thereof.

Isaiah 24:4-6

4 The *earth mourneth* and fadeth away, the world languisheth and fadeth away, the haughty people of the earth do languish.

5 The earth also is defiled under the inhabitants thereof; because they have transgressed the laws, changed the ordinance, broken the everlasting covenant.

6 Therefore hath the curse devoured the earth, and they that dwell therein are desolate: therefore the inhabitants of the earth are burned, and few men left. KJV

Isaiah 24:19-20

19 The earth is utterly **broken down,**

the earth is clean **dissolved,**
the earth is **moved exceedingly.**

20 The earth shall **reel to and fro like a drunkard,**
and shall be **removed** like a cottage;
and the transgression thereof shall be heavy upon it;and **it shall fall,**
and **not rise again.** KJV

By considering Old Testament imagery, it aids us in deciphering the objective of passages such as 2 Peter 3:10. The scriptures flow in total conformity with patterns initiated in the earliest writings of covenant man. The passage would be inconsistent with prophetic tradition if one insists that these apparent cosmological references articulate the destruction of the cosmos as we know it. Its use in the modern apocalyptic motif is essentially a break from the hermeneutical blueprint established by the Prophets that preceded Peter. The continued violation of these established patterns caused a great amount of confusion regarding eschatology and the spurious expectations of the "Left Behind" movement.

2 Peter 3:10

10 But the day of the Lord will come as a thief in the night;
-in the which **the heavens** shall pass away with a great noise, and
- the elements shall melt with fervent heat, the earth also and
-**the works** that are therein shall be burned up. KJV

Chapter 3
The Light in a Dark Place

To determine the objectives of Genesis One, we should examine the method by which the author defined the principle components of the text. The preconceived notions of cosmology have dominated the religious scene and have inadvertently forced their modern analysis upon an ancient narrative that was never initially intended. The first component introduced into the creation motif is that of light.

Genesis 1:3-4

3 And God said, Let there be light: and there was light. KJV

4 And God saw the light, that it was good: and God divided the light from the darkness. KJV

Genesis 1:3-4

and "Elohiym [Powers]" said, light exist and light existed and "Elohiym [Powers] " saw the light given that it was functional and "Elohim [Powers] made a separation between light and darkness.
Mechanical Translation of the Book of Genesis p.15

A question seldom raised about this passage concerns the nature of this "light." Traditionally, the knee-jerk response to the question of light in Genesis One verse three would be the cosmic light of our universe. Is this what the author of Genesis intended for his audience or does this documentation of light on the first creative day possess greater consequences? We believe that the proper definition of light in this passage gives us the first clue as to the disposition of the entire text and its message. Once we ascertain the character of the text, i.e., prophetic, poetic, or historical, then we may confidently approach its content in its native tongue. There must be a continuity of intent by its author and a perception of that intent by his audience. The author of Genesis defined the nature and function of **light** and revealed it as a **measure of time**; it is called day. The **darkness** he defined as a **measure of time** called the night. The scripture proceeds in verse five to define and identify the evening and the morning as the first day.

Light = day
Darkness = Night
Evening + Morning = 1st day

Genesis 1:5

5 And God called **the light Day**, and **the darkness he called Night**. And the **evening and the morning were the first day**. KJV

Genesis 1:5
and "Elohim [Powers]" called out to the light day and to the darkness he called out night and the evening existed and the morning existed one day.
Mechanical Version of Genesis

At this juncture, the introduction of assumed cosmic time is quite telling in spite of its complete lack of usage in the prophetic narratives of the Biblical record. John

Walton makes this observation in his groundbreaking book, "The Lost World of Genesis One"...

"Now comes the clincher. If "light" refers to a period of light in verse 5 and verse 4, consistency demands that we extend the same understanding to verse 3...We are compelled by the demands of verse 4 and 5 to translate verse 3 as "God said, 'Let there be a period of light.'"
John H. Walton. "The Lost World of Genesis One." InterVarsity Press, Page 54.

Walton appears to view this as a period of chronological time; however, he never makes the quantum leap of declaring the obvious. He rightly observes that Genesis One is not at all about cosmology, but he fails to recognize the prophetic nature of the text. If indeed he does perceive this exposition, it is not stated clearly in his writing. The continued prophetic assumptions of this pattern evidenced in:

Isaiah 42:16:

16 And I will bring the blind by a way that they knew not; I will lead them in paths that they have not known: **I will make darkness light before them,** and crooked things straight. These things will I do unto them, and not forsake them. KJV

The light/darkness motif initiated in the earliest parts of Genesis consistently demonstrates its prophetic occupation in time and space within the framework of covenantal events. The importance of this fact should not be understated. The passage: **"And God said, Let there be"** introduced the simple fact that the overall nature of the word of God is prophetic. All who pursue the study of holy writ should understand that it is a progressive prophecy from Genesis to the book of Revelation. The accuracy of what we have stated here is well supported and confirmed in 2 Peter Chapter One. The allusion to Genesis One with its prophetic underpinnings is identifiable.

2 Peter 1: 16, 19-21

16 For we have not followed cunningly devised fables, when we made known unto you the power and coming of our Lord Jesus Christ, but were eyewitnesses of his majesty.

19 We have also a more sure word of prophecy; whereunto ye do well that ye take heed, **as unto a light that shineth in a dark place**, until **the day dawn**, and the day star arise in your hearts:

20 Knowing this first, that no prophecy of the scripture is of any private interpretation.

21 For **the prophecy** came not in old time by the will of man: but holy men of God spake as they were moved by the Holy Ghost. KJV

The apostle Peter was alluding to the consummating events that disclosed the vision of the transfiguration where Moses and Elijah discussed the general resurrection with Jesus (Luke 9:31). Most analysts view this discussion as only concerning the "decease" or the crucifixion and death of Christ. According to Peter, the context of that conversation pertained to "the power and coming of our Lord Jesus Christ" (vs. 16) and not only his death. The text in the KJV utilizes the word "decease," but the Greek renders the word "exodon" (Exodus). On another occasion, the New Testament refers to the directive of Joseph concerning his bones when the children of Israel were departing (exodon) from Egypt (Hebrews 11:22).

We should also note that Revelation 11:8 refers to Jerusalem as "Egypt," thus the parallel is firmly established between what Jesus accomplished in Jerusalem (Egypt) and the historical exodus of the Hebrew children from the clutches of Pharaoh king of Egypt. It is noteworthy that both the Passover that initiated the Hebrew exodus and the death, burial, and resurrection of Jesus initiated two forty-year eras that culminated in the consummation of their respective kingdoms. The bones of Joseph traveled with the twelve tribes for forty years until they reached the land flowing 3with milk and honey. The bones of Joseph signified a future fulfillment of the righteous dead entering into its final destination at the end of the first forty-year period of church history. The passage clarifies the presence of Moses and Elijah in the narrative of the Transfiguration; they were about to embrace their eternal reward. Additionally, the "type" of Israel's "exodus' out of Egypt dovetails with the characterization of Jerusalem as "Sodom and Egypt." The twin narratives of Joseph's bones reaching the Promised Land after 40 years and the Lord leading the righteous dead into their celestial abode at the end of 40 years are more than coincidental.

Revelation 11:8

And their dead bodies *shall lie* in the street of the great city, which spiritually is called Sodom and Egypt, where also our Lord was crucified. KJV

Although the transfiguration was indeed a magnificent event, Peter admonished his audience that they possessed "a more sure word of prophecy," i.e., something more convincing than the related event of the Transfiguration, and that was the prophetic word of God. Peter uses the words "light in a dark place" and "until the DAY dawn." Both phrases are rooted in the Genesis One account and for a good reason. The re-creation of Israel was about to occur in their lifetime, and the prophetic fulfillment of the transition from night to day was upon them. The prophetic seventh day was about to dawn before their eyes. This position is also expressed eloquently by the apostle Paul to the Romans, for the prophetic day of deliverance was at hand. The expression "far spent" refers to the waxing away of the old covenant and the bringing forth of the _day_ when no night exists for the Church.

Romans 13:11-12

11 And that, knowing the time, that **now** it is high time to awake out of sleep: for now is our salvation nearer than when we believed.

12 **The night** is far spent, **the day** is at hand: let us therefore cast off the works of darkness, and let us put on the armour of light.

13 Let us walk honestly, _as in the day_; not in rioting and drunkenness, not in chambering and wantonness, not in strife and envying. KJV

Additional references that attest to this awareness are manifold in the sacred text. The urgency of its statement denotes imminence as to its advent. The Apostle Paul clearly understood the prophetic time in which he lived. The Apostle John concurred in agreement when he penned the following passage:

Revelation 22:4-5

4. And they shall see his face; and his name _shall be_ in their foreheads.

5 And there _shall be no night there;_ and they need no candle, neither light of the sun; for the Lord God giveth them light: and they shall reign for ever and ever. KJV

Isaiah also chimes in to support this narrative as the new covenant forecasted with the identical language of Genesis One and Two as it brings the creative week into its cessation in the seventh day as its pattern of works brought into its final rest.

Isaiah 60:19-20

19 The sun shall be no more thy light by day; neither for brightness shall the moon give light unto thee: but the Lord shall be unto thee an everlasting light, and thy God thy glory.

20 Thy sun shall no more go down; neither shall thy moon withdraw itself: for the Lord shall be thine everlasting light, and the days of thy mourning shall be ended. KJV

If the usage of the words "day" and "night" are not alluding to a 24-hour cycle, then what was Paul teaching? His audience was familiar with these terms because he used them in a traditionally established prophetic voice. His message was not an ambiguous warning but one by which the hearers readily acknowledged its imagery through the Old Testament writings. Additionally, this admonition from the Apostle makes a powerful relationship to the day and night prototype established in Genesis One. We should note here that the beginning of each day in Israel commenced in the evening. The association of darkness/evening is introduced before the mention of light or day in verse two, "...and there was darkness upon the face of the deep..." Therefore the identification of darkness and light initiated a pattern used to contrast the condition of man's spiritual status regarding his covenantal relationship with God. The correlation of light and day, darkness and night, should also be evaluated in conjunction with its prophetic value, as we have mentioned earlier in this writing. The use of this imagery in the New Testament is in the writings of the Apostle John. John never used the terms of light and darkness in terms of cosmic timekeeping but rather in terms of covenant relationship. When we reconsider John 3:19-20 because of Genesis One, the covenant implications of the following passages are truly astonishing.

John 3:19-21

19 And this is the condemnation, that *light* is come into the world, and men loved *darkness* rather than *light*, because their deeds were evil.

20 For every one that doeth evil hateth the *light*, neither cometh to the *light* , lest his deeds should be reproved.

21 But he that doeth truth cometh to the *light*, that his deeds may be made manifest, that they are wrought in God. KJV

John 12:46 is presented in the same way. Light is introduced as covenant redemption to those who embrace it.

John 12:46

46 I am come a light into the world, that whosoever believeth on me should not abide in darkness KJV

The cyclical pattern of man's inconsistent relationship with God illustrated in the creation/decreation themes found throughout the Bible. The compassion of God consistently demonstrates his willingness to replicate the process of regeneration in spite of Israel's horrid condition. The mutual relationship of the creation account (Day) in Genesis One and the darkness of decreation (Night) vividly portrayed in the following scripture. Note how verse 22 addressed the backslidden condition of Israel and reiterates that statement in verse 23 (Hebrew Parallelism) as it proceeds with the pre-creation imagery of Genesis 1: 2 in Jeremiah 4:22-27

22 For my people is foolish, they have not known me; they are sottish children, and they have none understanding: they are wise to do evil, but to do good they have no knowledge.
KJV
23 I beheld the earth, and, lo, it was without form, and void; and the heavens, and they had no light.

24 I beheld the mountains, and, lo, they trembled, and all the hills moved lightly.

25 I beheld, and, lo, **there was no man, and all the birds of the heavens were fled.** (Gen. 2:5)

26 I beheld, and, lo, **the fruitful place was a wilderness**, and all the cities thereof were broken down at the presence of the Lord, and by his fierce anger.

27 For thus hath the Lord said, **The whole land shall be desolate**; yet will I not make a full end. KJV

The portrayal of covenantal accountability is consistently depicted in this manner as through the eviction of God's posterity as a kingdom in ruin. The same imagery is evoked approximately one hundred years earlier with the threat of an Assyrian invasion from the north (Isaiah 8:21-22). The displacement of Israel through the Assyrian and Babylonian invasions is a reoccurring motif of the prototype of Adam's eviction from the presence of the Lord. The loss of sovereignty through the dominance of the Philistines also adds a kind of cadence to the travail experienced by Israel in its long struggle to survive as a people. Thus, the Day/Night and Light/Darkness theme play itself out as it assumes various forms and expressions throughout Holy Writ.

Isaiah 8:21-22

21 And they shall pass through it, hardly bestead and hungry: and it shall come to pass, that when they shall be hungry, they shall fret themselves, and curse their king and their God, and look upward.

22 And they shall look unto the earth; and behold trouble and darkness, dimness of anguish; and they shall be driven to darkness.

The relationship between the Day and Night is governed by God's covenantal ordinances delineated in Genesis One. The fourth day of creation (Genesis 1:14-18) illustrates the function of the greater and lesser lights that were to rule and divide light on the earth. Furthermore, its function was also to regulate the prophetic signs and seasons through its cycles of days and years. This function was manifested through the Feasts of Israel as an agricultural pattern as it designated prophetic events to be fulfilled "in their seasons." The Feasts of Israel were the heartbeat of Jewish religious activity without which they would cease to be a people because it defined and coordinated all their covenant activities concerning worship, and ultimately, their destiny. The importance of this illustrated in the following texts, which have their extraction from Genesis One. The language utilized in these passages are indicative of the associations between light/day; / darkness/night regarding Israel's covenant destiny as opposed to the universal cosmic order.

Covenant of the Day and the Covenant of the Night

The pattern of Day and Night developed into multiples of weeks, months, and years in the 14th verse of Genesis One. The heavenly bodies of the sun, moon, and stars, function in prophetic harmony to rightly divide the Day and Night for signs, seasons, days and years. The word "seasons" is rendered "Moed," or convocations in Hebrew, the appointed fulfillment for Israel's eternal destiny. The pattern was codified on Mt. Sinai through its agricultural system of feasts as they functioned in types and shadows, awaiting their fulfillment. The covenant of Day and Night alluded to below refers to this prophetic/sacrificial system. The old covenant was synchronized and governed by this sacrificial system and called *the Feasts of the Lord*. The covenant and its prophetic system were inseparable. One element could not survive without the other, or they would cease to exist. Israel's identification with that system of worship tied them to an expectation of fulfillment for every promise made to their posterity.

Jeremiah 31:35-37

35 Thus saith the Lord, which giveth the sun for a light by day, and the ordinances of the moon and of the stars for a light by night, which divideth the sea when the waves thereof roar; The Lord of hosts is his name:

36 If those ordinances depart from before me, saith the Lord, then the seed of Israel also shall cease from being a nation before me for ever.

37 Thus saith the Lord; If heaven above can be measured, and the foundations of the earth searched out beneath, I will also cast off all the seed of Israel for all that they have done, saith the Lord.

Jeremiah 33:20-21

20 Thus saith the Lord; **If ye can break my covenant of the day, and my covenant of the night, and that there should not be day and night in their season; (appointed times)**

21 Then may also my covenant be broken with David my servant, that he should not have a son to reign upon his throne; and with the Levites the priests, my ministers. KJV

Jeremiah 33:23-26

23 Moreover, the word of the Lord came to Jeremiah, saying,

24 Have you not noticed that these people [the Jews] are saying, The Lord has cast off the two families [Israel and Judah] which He chose? Thus my people have despised [themselves in relation to God as His covenant people], so that they are no more a nation in their [own] sight.
25 Thus says the Lord: If **My covenant with day and night** does not stand, and if I have not appointed the ordinances of the heavens and the earth,

26 Then will I also cast away the descendants of Jacob and David My servant and will not choose one of his offspring to be ruler over the descendants of Abraham, Isaac, and Jacob. For I will cause their captivity to be reversed, and I will have mercy, kindness, and steadfast love on and for them. [Genesis 49:10.] AMP

The day and night prophetic motif established in Genesis One expressed its judgment of the night in Amos 5:18-20. All prophecy concerning judgment seems to find its roots in the obscurity of prophetic darkness established in Genesis One.

Amos 5:18-20

18 Woe to you who long or the day of the Lord!
Why do you long for the day of the Lord?
That day will be darkness, not light.
19 It will be as though a man fled from a lion
only to meet a bear, as though he entered his house
and rested his hand on the wall only to have a snake bite him.
20 Will not **the day of the Lord be darkness, not light pitch-dark, without a ray of brightness?** NIV

Revelation 16:10

10 And the fifth angel poured out his vial upon the seat of the beast; **and his kingdom was full of darkness;** and they gnawed their tongues for pain, KJV

Nahum 1:8

8 But with an overrunning flood he will make an utter end of the place thereof, and **darkness shall pursue his enemies**. KJV

It also depicts the recreation of the new heavens and earth but now without the need of these heavenly bodies because of their fulfillment. Jesus hinted at this new designation when he said to his disciples. "Ye are the light of the world."

Revelation 21:22-25

22 And I saw no temple therein: for the Lord God Almighty and the Lamb are the temple of it.

23 And the city had no need of the sun, neither of the moon, to shine in it: for the glory of God did lighten it, and **the Lamb is the light thereof**.

24 And the nations of them which are saved **shall walk in the light of it**: and the kings of the earth do bring their glory and honour into it.

25 And the gates of it shall not be shut at all by day: for **there shall be no night there**. KJV

Amos preached regarding the judgment on the ten northern tribes of Israel. Note the darkening of the earth at noon. The event did not historically occur as superficially depicted but its prediction was the coming invasion by the Assyrians.

The imagery of darkness in the middle of the afternoon depicted a sort of "decreation." The theme recurs throughout scripture to relay a comparable message of judgment to covenant nations. The withdrawal of God's favor depicted in the prophetic writ is the removal of "light'. Usually, it involves an illustration of heavenly bodies.

Amos 8:9-10

9 "In that day," declares the Sovereign Lord,
"I will make the **sun go down at noon**
and darken the earth in broad daylight.
10 I will turn your religious feasts (The Feasts of Israel) into mourning and all your singing into weeping. NIV

Children of the Day and Children of the Light

1 Thessalonians chapter five demonstrates a strong association with Genesis One within its eschatological discourse mixed with comfort and warnings of impending wrath. The passage contains features of the creation narrative in association with God's people. Its apparent allusion to Genesis One would render it completely incompatible if the creation story were merely cosmological. Comprehending a relationship between natural light and spiritual light would be confusing when attempting to make a point of a covenantal nature. The prophetic nature of the text should indicate that the words **day** and **light** are defined when associated with their initial introduction into the text, that is to say, with their first mention in Genesis One. The phrase, "children of the

day" may be restated by saying, "children of the prophetic day" because that is precisely the relationship that Paul is making in the passage. Paul was fully cognizant of what he was communicating, given the language he used in the passage. Please note the usage of the word "seasons" as an express association to Genesis 1:14.

1 Thessalonians 5:1-2,4-8

5:1 But of *the times and the seasons*, brethren, ye have no need that I write unto you.

2 For yourselves know perfectly that the day of the Lord so cometh as a thief in the night.

3 For when they shall say, Peace and safety; then sudden destruction cometh upon them, as travail upon a woman with child; and they shall not escape.

4 But ye, brethren, are not in darkness, that that *day* should overtake you as a thief.
5 Ye are all the *children of light*, and the *children of the day*: we are not of the night, nor of *darkness*.

6 Therefore let us not sleep, as do others; but let us watch and be sober.
7 For they that sleep sleep in the night; and they that be drunken are drunken in the night.
8 But let *us, who are of the day*, be sober, putting on the breastplate of faith and love; and for an helmet, the hope of salvation. KJV

Paul's correlation of the fourth day of creation as recorded in Genesis 1: 14-18, and 1 Thessalonians 5:1 is a stroke of anointed genius. He was keenly aware of the language he used when discussing the coming of the Lord in that passage. The usage of the words "times and seasons" further acknowledged its prophetic relationship with the convocations of Israel and its "end-time fulfillment." These appointed times were later called the Feasts of the Lord (Leviticus 23:2) as they foreshadowed the events that transpired at the advent of the infant Church. The Church was made to know the timing of the outpouring of the Holy Ghost as Jesus also cautioned his followers *after* a request for the renewal of *their* kingdom (Israel). Jesus responded, "It is not for you to know the *times or the seasons* which the father has put in. his power"

Acts 1:6-8

6 When they therefore were come together, they asked of him, saying, Lord, wilt thou at this time restore again the kingdom to Israel?

7 And he said unto them, It is not for you to know the times or the seasons, which the Father hath put in his own power.

8 But ye shall receive power, after that the Holy Ghost is come upon you: and ye shall be witnesses unto me both in Jerusalem, and in all Judæa, and in Samaria, and unto the uttermost part of the earth
Genesis1:14-18

14 And God saith, 'Let luminaries be in the expanse of the heavens, to make a separation between the day and the

night, then they have been for *signs, and for seasons, and for days and years,*

15 and they have been for luminaries in the expanse of the heavens to give light upon the earth:' and it is so.

16 And God maketh the two great luminaries (*light*), the great luminary for the *rule of the day*, and the small luminary (*light*) — and the stars — for the *rule of the night*;

17 and God giveth them in the expanse of the heavens to give light upon the earth,

18 and *to rule over day and over night, and to make a separation between the light and the darkness*; and God seeth that [it is] good; YLT

The expression, "We are children of the light and the children of the day" (1 Thes.5:5) identifies the Church with the prophetic day of Genesis One. We must, therefore, remember that the light ruled or regulated the prophetic day. The word 'rule" is defined as dominion or domain just as a kingdom rules its subjects. On the other hand, Paul also stated that "We are not of the night or darkness." The designation of that statement disassociates the church from the lesser light that ruled the night because it is indicative of life before Christ. Jews under the Law ruled by the lesser light. It is not a matter of happenstance that the moon regulated the
ceremonial appointments of the feasts, which were only a reflection of things to come. As Genesis 1:14 stated, the light of the sun, moon, and the stars were also the function of prophecy that was for signs, seasons, days, and years.

The prophetic significance of Genesis 1:14 administrated the festivals in sequence as Israel choreographed its agricultural types and shadows year in and year out.

Day four, as the other days of creation, entered into its Sabbath on the seventh day when the focal point of its worship and service (the Temple) the Romans destroyed in 70 A.D. Paul admonished the church of Galatia not to return to the worship of his forefathers and likened it to bondage (slavery).

Galatians 4:9-10

9 But now, after that ye have known God, or rather are known of God, how turn ye again to the weak and beggarly elements, whereunto ye desire again to be in bondage?

10 Ye observe **days, and months, and times, and years**. KJV

Paul understood that the days of the shadow were quickly coming to a close, and its fulfillment was nigh at hand.
Colossian 2:16-17

16 Let no one, then, judge you in eating or in drinking, or in respect of a feast, or of a new moon, or of sabbaths,

17 which are a shadow of the coming things, and the body [is] of the Christ; YLT

More usage of the Prophetic Day

In warning of apostate teachers, Peter referred to them as "natural brute beasts," thus depicting a disruptive movement within the Church by unruly members. Verse 13 further portrays their activities as those who **"riot in the day time."** The prophetic day of the new covenant Church is also depicted by the Apostle Paul many times throughout his writings. Both Romans 13:13 and 2 Peter 2:12-13 are good illustrations of this method of prophetic articulation by these beloved Apostles.

2 Peter 2:12-13

12 But these, as natural brute beasts, made to be taken and destroyed, speak evil of the things that they understand not; and shall utterly perish in their own corruption;

13 And shall receive the reward of unrighteousness, as they that count it pleasure to **riot in the day time**. Spots they are and blemishes, sporting themselves with their deceivings while they feast with you; KJV

 Romans 13:13

13 Let us walk honestly, **as in the day**; not in rioting and drunkenness, not in chambering and wantonness, not in strife and envying. KJV

Chosen and Called Through the Light

The prophetic light of the gospel preached by Christ foretold in Isaiah 9:2-3 and speaks of its fulfillment in Luke 2:32. The language of covenant creation is vividly presented here with Genesis One imagery. Verse three reflects the joy of the Holy Ghost and the nation enlarged with the redemption of God's people with the demonstration of new power in the renewed kingdom, the redemption of God's people.

Isaiah 9:2-3

2 The people walking in darkness have seen a great light; those living in the land of the shadow of death a light has dawned.
3 You have enlarged the nation and increased their joy; they rejoice before you as people rejoice at the harvest, as men rejoice when dividing the plunder. NIV

Light is also a recurring theme throughout the entire New Testament narrative. Rarely is it rendered as natural or cosmological. The blinding light of the Mount of Transfiguration is one infrequent example that immediately comes to mind. The covenant theme of light, resurrection, and new life are patterns that need close examination when reviewing passages such as these. These texts sourced from Genesis One in sentiment and prophetic application, but the skewed orientation of religious dogma forbids the consideration of such an association. The treasures revealed within that relationship unleashes a flood gate of understanding that is well worth the raised eyebrows of disbelieving brethren and the harsh criticism of religious systems. The call of God through the anointed word impels every willing believer into the presence of His kingdom. The incessant repetition of the narrative of redemption, the "born again" experience, and its relationship to the church within the day/ light motif reveal its importance to us as it urges its patterns to be understood.

1 Peter 2:9-10

9 But ye are a chosen generation, a royal priesthood, an holy nation, a peculiar people; that ye should shew forth the praises of him who hath *called you out of darkness into his marvellous light:*

10 Which in time past were not a people, but are now the people of God: which had not obtained mercy, but now have obtained mercy.

Colossians 1:12-13

12 Giving thanks unto the Father, which hath made us meet to be partakers of the inheritance of the saints in light:

13 Who hath *delivered us from the power of darkness, and hath translated us into the kingdom* of his dear Son...

Chapter 4

The Wisdom of Creation

The first six days and their moral teaching

The metaphoric relationships that are made between light and darkness, day and night, etc. were defined by their meticulous separations or divisions. These divisions essentially provide the structured formulation of boundaries that convey the unique birthing of life forms out of the mass of confusion first illustrated in Genesis 1:2.

- The principle properties of day one reiterated in day four by the **division** of light and darkness, thus the creation of prophetic time and its luminaries; Sun, Moon, and Stars.
- The waters of days two and five are **separated** as it yielded creatures of the sea as portrayed in Mathew 13:47
- The **separation** of the waters and the dry land in days three and six yielded man and beast.

The narrative of separation developed very early on in scripture as it emphasized a moral discourse that the ancients clearly understood. Covenant life is initiated and maintained through a series of divisions and separations unto the covenant state. The prototype of the call of God to covenant believers noted in the call of Abraham in Genesis 12. Abraham was challenged to make radical departures from the mores of his family, culture, and lifestyle before his journey to Canaan. The separation he made was much more than a relocation of his assets. It required a total reevaluation of his priorities and values that set in motion the destiny of a people throughout all the ages.

Genesis 12:1-2

1 Now the Lord had said unto Abram, Get thee out of thy country, and from thy kindred, and from thy father's house, unto a land that I will shew thee:

2 And I will make of thee a great nation, and I will bless thee, and make thy name great; and thou shalt be a blessing: KJV

The cyclical drama of separation and inclusion from and into the world around God's people continues even to this day. The human proclivity for failure in maintaining the boundaries of covenant life abounds in scripture.

....

*"*An ancient reader would find the text of Genesis inseparable from the moral teachings of the Bible.* The creation story, especially in its earliest narratives, is rhetorical more so than it is historical in nature. The act of God dividing light from darkness, day from night, heaven from the deep, earth from the sea, heaven from earth, is a moral matter. How would an ancient reader automatically know this, when we do not? It is because, to the ancient reader, the act of dividing and the act of wise discernment are exactly the same thing. When the ancient reader read, "God divided the light from the darkness" in his language, the action was represented in two parts. Just as we in English say: "God **divided** x **from** y,"*

145

"And God **(he) divides between** x and **between** y."

- The verb representing the action of dividing is
בדל **"badal**," Strong's #914 [1]. The term denoting which
things are being separated, i.e. "between," is בין **"beyn**,"
Strong's   #996

Exo 26:33 And thou shalt hang up the vail under the
taches, that thou mayest bring in thither within the vail the
ark of the testimony: and the vail shall **divide (badal)**
unto you **between (beyn)** the holy *place* and the most
holy.

Lev 10:10 And that ye may **put difference (badal)**
between holy and unholy, and **between (beyn)** unclean
and clean;
....

"God separated light from darkness, God separated
waters from waters, and God separated holy from unholy.
Does that really mean that there is necessarily a
relationship tying all of those acts together, apart from the
fact that the same word structure was used to convey the
ideas? With these passages alone, we are only left with a
curious tendency wherein we might notice some vague
correlation. Fuel for conjecture, maybe, but nothing
profound or solid would be yielded from it.
However, the story does not end here for the ancient
reader. For the ancient reader, the latter term also had a
usage on its own [3]. This usage referred to the act or
ability to divide - that is, discern - between two or more
things on an issue: Good and evil, justice and injustice,
etc. How do we render this ability in English?

Wisdom, knowledge, understanding, perception and discernment. The word also applies to **instruction** - that is, teaching a student how to discern."

"In the Bible, "wisdom" or "understanding" is the ability to __divide__ good from evil, righteousness from unrighteousness, and is expressed with the same word used to express God's dividing light "from" darkness."

Hebrews 4:12-13

12 For the word of God *is* quick, and powerful, and sharper than any two-edged sword, piercing even to the dividing asunder of soul and spirit, and of the joints and marrow, and *is* a discerner of the thoughts and intents of the heart.

13 Neither is there any creature that is not manifest in his sight: but all things *are* naked and opened unto the eyes of him with whom we have to do. KJV

Deu 1:13 Take you wise men, and **understanding**, and known among your tribes, and I will make them rulers over you.
"These passages go further to give us another dimension of deciphering the relationship between the physical act of division and the moral/intellectual act of discernment, but how do they connect this usage with Gen One in solidarity? This little word בדל is also a basis for larger words, denoting nuances of the same idea of discernment, cunning, and wisdom. One such term is תבונה "tebunah," Strong's #8394.[5] It is with this term that Solomon remarks of creation: Proverbs 3:13, 18-20

13 Happy *is* the man *that* findeth wisdom, and the man *that* getteth **understanding**.
...

18 She *is* a tree of life to them that lay hold upon her: and happy *is every one* that retaineth her
19 The LORD by wisdom hath founded the earth; by <u>understanding</u> hath he established the heavens.
20 By his knowledge the depths are broken up, and the clouds   drop   down   the   dew."
Dividing Heaven and Earth, Mathew McNabb, 2015

■ ....

The allusions to the Genesis narrative are pervasive as wisdom plays a prominent role in the propagation of covenant life. The prophetic function of the word wisdom in the book of Proverbs is arresting as it speaks to us in the first person. This personification of the word "wisdom" plays a major role in the very first chapter of Proverbs.

The Word of God and Wisdom are used interchangeably as performing corresponding functions of "creation" or Bara within a structured kingdom. Thus, their combined usage in passages regarding the building, strengthening, and restoration of its covenant constituency effectively portrays the same narrative as in Genesis One. Its voice is none other than the spirit of God working to and through covenant children. The voice of God and the voice of the Word inherently possess the same qualities as both merges in the purpose of structuring the covenant economy.

The converse of this personification is demonstrated by the following scripture, where the portrayal of two types of women in personification by playing opposing roles in the covenant economy. The Woman building her house in Proverbs 14:1 is doing so through the use of wisdom. Building **"her** house" is a reference to God's house. "The foolish" woman also portrayed as Israel, rebuked for her lawlessness, and as Jesus prophesied: "Behold, **your** house is left unto you desolate" (Matt. 23:38). It helps to support our contention that the building of God's house in Genesis chapters 1 and 2 is complementary to the functions and values of Proverbs 14:1. It is through the demarcations decreed in Genesis One, Proverbs, and many other similar passages throughout the Bible that reaffirm indistinguishable narratives.

Proverbs 14:1

14 Every wise woman buildeth her house: but the foolish plucketh it down with her hands. KJV

The call of discipleship through the beckoning of wisdom and understanding in Proverbs 8 illustrates quite vividly the wooing of a God to his people. The first four verses incorporate the familiar narrative of creation: the call out of spiritual darkness and the propagation of covenant creatures. The union of these ideas is not inconsequential as they are woven together in such a familiar way.

Doth not wisdom cry? and understanding put forth her voice?

2 She standeth in the top of high places, by the way in the places of the paths.

3 She crieth at the gates, at the entry of the city, at the coming in at the doors.

4 Unto you, O men, I call; and my voice *is* to the sons of man.

22 The Lord possessed me in the beginning of his way, before his works of old.

23 I was set up from everlasting, from the beginning, or ever the earth was.

24 When *there were* no depths, I was brought forth; when *there were* no fountains abounding with water.

25 Before the mountains were settled, before the hills was I brought forth:

26 While as yet he had not made the earth, nor the fields, nor the highest part of the dust of the world.

27 When he prepared the heavens, I *was* there: when he set a compass upon the face of the depth:

28 When he established the clouds above: when he strengthened the fountains of the deep:

29 When he gave to the sea his decree, that the waters should not pass his commandment: when he appointed the foundations of the earth:

30. Then I was by him, *as* one brought up *with him*: and I was daily *his* delight, rejoicing always before him;

31 Rejoicing in the habitable part of his earth; and my delights *were* with the sons of men.

32 Now therefore hearken unto me, O ye children: for blessed *are they that* keep my ways.

The Pillars of Our Covenant World

The significance of the seven pillars of Proverbs 9:1 is a mystery for many students of scripture. The usual guesswork employs an attempt to decipher its suggestions. Its secrets reveal through an understanding of what the word *seven* represents in the imagery of prophetic word speak. The feeble attempt of employing a literal "seven" to a patently prophetic expression is a sure-fire way of destroying the passage. Strong's does admit that **sheba (seven)** can denote an indefinite number. We believe that in this case, it attests to this word's prophetic value as opposed to its cardinal value of simply the number seven. Additional evidence that compliments this view is that the word "pillar" is closely associated with the Church in typology. Pillars support God's greatest creation through the "hewn" process of the Word. The house that wisdom builds has an innumerable constituency. This constituency is "hewn" to the specifications of its builder and maker. Furthermore, its inference to cutting corresponds to Bara (creation) in that Bara also has the same designation as "hewn" in Hebrew lexicons. The sacrificial designations of this passage are apparent as the mention of bread and wine speaks volumes to the sacrificial order of that house.

OT:2672 Hewn:

chatsab (khaw-tsab'); or **chatseb** (khaw-tsabe'); a primitive root to cut or carve (wood), stone or other material); by implication, to hew, split, square, quarry, engrave:

KJV - cut, dig, divide, grave, hew (out, -er), made, mason.

(Biblesoft's New Exhaustive Strong's Numbers and Concordance with Expanded Greek-Hebrew Dictionary. Copyright © 1994, 2003, 2006 Biblesoft, Inc. and International Bible Translators, Inc.)

Proverbs 9:1-6

1. Wisdom hath built her house, she hath hewn out her seven pillars:

2 She hath killed her beasts; she hath mingled her wine; she hath also furnished her table.

3 She hath sent forth her maidens: she crieth upon the highest places of the city,

4 Whoso *is* simple, let him turn in hither: *as for* him that wanteth understanding, she saith to him,

5 Come, eat of my bread, and drink of the wine *which* I have mingled.

6 Forsake the foolish, and live; and go in the way of understanding. KJV

OT:7651 ub^v# **sheba`** (sheh'-bah); or (masculine) **shib`ah** (shib-aw'); from OT:7650; a primitive cardinal number; seven (as the sacred full one); also (adverbially) seven times; by implication, a week; by extension, **an** **indefinite** **number**:

(Biblesoft's New Exhaustive Strong's Numbers and Concordance with Expanded Greek-Hebrew Dictionary. Copyright © 1994, 2003, 2006 Biblesoft, Inc. and International Bible Translators, Inc.)

Revelation 3:12

12 Him that overcometh will I make a pillar in the temple of my God, and he shall go no more out: and I will write upon him the name of my God, and the name of the city of my God, *which is* New Jerusalem, KJV

Pillars under the Altar

A surprising source of this pattern is found in Exodus 24:3-5. As we all know, nothing is left to chance in the Biblical record. The designation of the number 12 in scripture points to the sum of covenant believers. There are multiple references to "the twelve tribes of Israel" and to the multiplication of 12s, as expressed in Revelation 6:4 (144,000), where the sealing of the tribes of Israel points to the whole community of first-generation firstfruit believers. The imagery of the altar erected in the wilderness supported by 12 pillars speaks to the same narrative. The sacrificial image the Altar portrays is a type that embraces the entirety of Israel's constituents as they uphold the priestly order fulfilled in the New Testament called a "Holy Priesthood."

Exodus 24:3-5
3."Everything the LORD HAS said we will do."

4 Moses then wrote down everything the LORD HAD said.

He got up early the next morning and built an altar at the foot of the mountain and set up **twelve stone pillars representing the twelve tribes of Israel. NIV**

We would be remiss to evade the same imagery found in Revelation 6. The depiction of the souls slain for the word of God expresses the ultimate sacrifice paid by those who were undoubtedly pillars of the sacrificial order.

Revelation 6:9-11

9 And when he had opened the fifth seal, **I saw under the altar the souls of them that were slain for the word of God,** and for the testimony which they held:

10 And they cried with a loud voice, saying, How long, O Lord, holy and true, dost thou not judge and avenge our blood on them that dwell on the earth?

11 And white robes were given unto every one of them, and it was said unto them, that they should rest yet for a little season, until their fellow-servants also and their brethren, that should be killed as they *were*, should be fulfilled. KJV

The replication of this imagery is in 1Samuel 2:6-9 through the prophecy of Hanna in her prayer of thanksgiving to God for the birth of her son Samuel. Special note to the keywords in the passage to resurrection type language and its reference to "the pillars of the earth." Its relationship to Genesis 2:7 is also apparent in verse 8 in "He raiseth up the poor out of the dust..." covenantal themes abound here if one gives the slightest attention to its details. The poor and the beggar are taken from the dust/dunghill and placed among princes and inherit the throne of glory. The pillars are an extension of the prevailing theme of a constituency of covenant believers upholding the Kingdom of God (covenant world) and its truth.

1 Samuel 2:6-8

6 The Lord killeth, and maketh alive: he bringeth down to the grave, and bringeth up.

7 The Lord maketh poor, and maketh rich: he bringeth low, and lifteth up.

8 He raiseth up the poor out of the dust, *and* lifteth up the beggar from the dunghill, to set *them* among princes, and to make them inherit the throne of glory: for the pillars of the earth *are* the Lord's, and he hath set the world upon them. KJV

Decreation

When the distinctive parameters established by wisdom are blurred, unique characteristics of the covenant commence deteriorating. Nowhere in scripture is this better expressed than in Jeremiah 4:22-23 as verses 22 and 23 reiterate the same narrative about Israel in Hebrew parallelism. The demarcations that made them a people unto the Lord deteriorated into hopeless apostasy.

Jeremiah 4:22-23

22 "My people are fools; they do not know me.

They are senseless children; **they have no understanding**.

They are skilled in doing evil; they **know not how to do good**."

23 I looked at the earth, and it was formless and empty;

and at the heavens, and **their light was gone**. NIV (see Genesis 1:2)

The pursuit of wisdom, understanding, dividing, and separating within the context of Genesis One may now be associated with similar expressions in the New Testament to verify their pedigree as concerning their covenant implications.

Day One Out of Darkness

When determining their unique relationships, it is imperative to reinvestigate the merging narratives of the Old and New Testaments. The covenantal implications of Genesis 1:3-5 remains a mystery to New Testament exegesis, but we will endeavor to illustrate their kinship by allowing the scriptures to speak for themselves. As we have demonstrated in our chapter entitled "Light in a Dark Place," the cosmic view of the terms *Light* and *Day* fall woefully short of their perceived assumptions. Either there is harmony between the New and Old testaments as concerning the following passages or the Biblical narrative disintegrates into a conflict of unrelated patterns that are very difficult to justify hermeneutically.

Genesis 1:3-5

3 And God said, Let there be light: and there was light.

4 And God saw the light, that it was good: and God divided the light from the darkness.

5 And God called the light Day, and the darkness he called Night. And the evening and the morning were the first day KJV

2 Corinthians 4:6

6 For God, who commanded the light to shine out of darkness, hath shined in our hearts, to give the light of the knowledge of the glory of God in the face of Jesus Christ. KJV

Ephesians 5:8
8 For ye were sometimes darkness, but now are ye light in the Lord: walk as children of light KJV

-The Second Day: Through the Waters

Ascribing the preoccupation of worshipping heavens and the waters and waters above the waters in Psalms 148:4 is perplexing at best. The only way one may resolve the apparent absurdity of this expression is to consider its figurative relationship to Genesis 1:6-8. Both passages complement each other in form and content once their intrinsic values are made plain. There is no alternate scriptural reasoning for the way that Psalms 148:4 is presented in the text. Genesis One essentially serves as a proof text of similar "nonsensical" passages sprinkled throughout the Bible.

Genesis 1:6-8

6 And God said, Let there be a firmament in the midst of the waters, and let it divide the waters from the waters.

7 And God made the firmament, and divided the waters which were under the firmament from the waters which were above the firmament: and it was so.

Psalms 148:4

4 Praise him, ye heavens of heavens, and ye waters that *be* above the heavens. KJV

The covenant language of Genesis 1:6-8 is replicated at the onset of events in Exodus 14 when the Hebrew children pass through the Red sea in flight from the Egyptians. The picture of a divided sea depicts God's heavenly posterity passes through its waters. It effectively portrays a mirror image to the text on the second day of Genesis One. The firmament (or the heavens) is, in fact, in the midst of the waters of deliverance. This picture of redemption is unmistakable and found in the earliest portions of the ancient text. Thus, the portrayal of heavenly offspring in Psalms 78:12-13 first portrayed in Genesis 1:6-8.

Psalms 78:12-13

12 Marvellous things did he in the sight of their fathers, in the land of Egypt, in the field of Zoan.

13 He divided the sea , and caused them to pass through; and he made the waters to stand as an heap. KJV

Days 1 and 2

Exodus 14:20-22 gives us a panoramic overview of the first two days of Genesis One. It serves as a snapshot of the creation of Israel; a people birthed out of the midst of Egyptian bondage. The demarcation of Israel's new identity adjudicated on Mount Sinai; the identity of slavery thus eradicated. The wisdom of God's word thus created a new nation that reflected the character of the Father. Note the same elements of a division between light and darkness as Israel passes through a divided sea, creating dry land. It unquestionably parallels the Genesis One account. The destruction of Israel's enemies proved to be a fatal blow to the army of the Egyptians. This imagery concurs with the liberation of New Testament baptism as it parallels the bondage of sin destroyed just as the Hebrew children baptized unto Moses in the Red Sea. (Colossians 2:10-12)

Exodus 14:20-23

20 And it came between the camp of the Egyptians and the camp of Israel, and it was a cloud and darkness to them, but it gave **light by night** to these: so that the one came not near the other all the night.

21 And Moses stretched out his hand over the sea; and the Lord caused the sea to go back by a strong east wind all that night, and **made the sea dry land, and the waters were divided**.

22 And the children of Israel went into the midst of the sea upon the dry ground: and the waters were a wall unto them on their right hand, and on their left. KJV

23 And the Egyptians pursued, and went in after them to the midst of the sea, *even* all Pharaoh's horses, his chariots, and his horsemen. KJV

The Third Day: Resurrection

Genesis 1:9-11

9 And God said, Let the waters under the heaven be gathered together unto one place, and let the dry land appear: and it was so.

10 And God called the dry land Earth; and the gathering together of the waters called he the Seas: and God saw that it was good.

11 And God said, Let the earth bring forth grass, the herb yielding seed, and the fruit tree yielding fruit after his kind, whose seed is in itself, upon the earth: and it was so. KJV

The third day of creation portrays a type of resurrection;

the earth is a type of covenant man arisen with a bountiful expression of new life. The representation of Man as grass, trees, and an array of related agricultural life forms emerges out of the dry ground. The speculation is not on our part. The agricultural language of the New and Old Testaments utilizes the same language to portray new life in covenant terms. Furthermore, the typology of the risen Christ depicted as Christ, "the first fruits of them that slept" (1 Corinthians 15:20). The Bible also designates the first generation believers as "a kind of firstfruits."

James 1:18

18 Of his own will begat he us with the word of truth, that we should be a kind of firstfruits of his creatures. KJV

The Biblical personification of Israel as the Olive Tree, the Fig Tree, the choice vine, or as the grass of the field all depict the people of the covenant.

Isaiah 51:12

12 "I, even I, am he who comforts you. Who are you that you fear mortal men, the sons of men, who are but grass
Isaiah 55:12

12 For ye shall go out with joy, and be led forth with peace: the mountains and the hills shall break forth before you into singing, and all the trees of the field shall clap *their* hands. KJV

The first allusion to the expression "whose seed is in itself" in Genesis 1:11 finds a place in the New Testament

161

writings of the Apostle John in 1John 3:9-10. The covenantal implications of this idiom inculcated through the differentiation of God's seed and the seed of the devil. Genesis 3:15 also makes the same distinctions through its prophetic metaphors.

Genesis 1:11-13

11 And God said, Let the earth bring forth grass, the herb yielding seed, *and* the fruit tree yielding fruit after his kind, whose seed *is* in itself, upon the earth: and it was so.

12 And the earth brought forth grass, *and* herb yielding seed after his kind, and the tree yielding fruit, whose seed *was* in itself, after his kind: and God saw that *it was* good.

13 And the evening and the morning were the third day. KJV

1 John 3:9-10

9 No one who is born of God will continue to sin, because **God's seed remains in him;** he cannot go on sinning, because he has been born of God. 10 This is how we know who the children of God are and who the children of the devil are: Anyone who does not do what is right is not a child of God; nor is anyone who does not love his brother. NIV

162

John the Baptist railed at the religious world when he warned them of the impending judgment against them. God was to cut them down like a lumberjack a tree. His allusion to Israel as a Tree is unmistakable. Trees are personified as men or even as countries in "prophecy-speak." The pattern is well established in the Biblical record. Therefore the New Testament allusion to such a pattern should not surprise the more discerning readers.

Luke 3:9

9 And now also the axe is laid unto **the root of the trees**: every tree therefore which bringeth not forth good fruit is hewn down and cast into the fire. KJV

The following passage is a good illustration of nations symbolized as trees. The scripture begins with the kingdom of Assyria and then alludes to the other nations of its day by referring to Assyria as being above or greater than "all the trees of the field." Jesus used the same illustration with "The fowls of heaven" when referring to the influences of men in the kingdom (filling its branches; Mark 4:32). References to the beasts of the field are consistent with Genesis One in that it established the foundation for the "beasts as men" motif in scripture.

Ezekiel 31:3-6

3 Behold, the Assyrian *was* a cedar in Lebanon with fair branches, and with a shadowing shroud, and of an high stature; and his top was among the thick boughs.

4 The waters made him great, the deep set him up on high with her rivers running round about his plants, and sent out her little rivers unto all the trees of the field.

5 Therefore his height was exalted above all the trees of the field, and his boughs were multiplied, and his branches became long because of the multitude of waters, when he shot forth.

6 All the fowls of heaven made their nests in his boughs, and under his branches did all the beasts of the field bring forth their young, and under his shadow dwelt all great nations. KJV

The Fourth Day: Seasons

Day four introduces the prophetic calendar through the operation of the sun, moon, and stars for the dividing of prophetic time. The general misconception of this motif as representing a cosmic timepiece in the sky only detracts from its prevailing function as "times and seasons" throughout the balance of the biblical record. Genesis 1:14 lays the foundation of how Israel ordered its festivals as guided by the phases of the moon (Exodus 12:2). The "moed" or season served as the convocation of its people that served to foreshadow the events fulfilled in Israel's future.

We previously documented Israel's identification as the "sun, moon, and stars. Israel's position as the prophetic light to the world transitions to another nation to whom Jesus referred as "the light of the world". Prophetic light is uniquely the possession of all covenant people beginning in the Old Testament and ultimately conveyed to the New Testament Church.

The seasons (**kairos** in Greek, **mowed** in Hebrew) as referenced in the New Testament (1Thess.5:1, Acts 1:7) are notably prophetic in posture. When passages mention, "the seasons," it always refers to the fulfillment of the old Prophets and the types depicted in the Feasts of the Lord. We will delve more deeply into this most important subject in the chapter entitled, "The Feasts, a Pattern of Prophetic Events."

Genesis 1:14-16

14 And God said, Let there be **lights** in the firmament of the heaven to divide the day from the night; and let them be for **signs, and for seasons (MOWED), and for days, and years:**

15 And let them be for lights in the firmament of the heaven to give light upon the earth: and it was so.

16 And God made two great lights; the greater light to rule the day, and the lesser light to rule the night: he made the stars also. KJV

Psalms 104:19-21

19 He appointed the moon for **seasons** (mowed): the sun knoweth his going down.

20 Thou makest darkness, and it is night: wherein all the beasts of the forest do creep forth.

OT:4150 Season: mowed` (mo-ade'); or moed` (mo-ade');
or (feminine) mow`adah (2 Chronicles 8:13) (mo-aw-
daw'); from OT:3259; properly, an appointment, i.e. a
fixed time or season; specifically, **a festival**;
conventionally a year; by implication, an assembly (as
convened for a definite purpose); **technically the
congregation**; by extension, the place of meeting; also a
signal (as appointed beforehand):

(Biblesoft's New Exhaustive Strong's Numbers and Concordance with
Expanded Greek-Hebrew Dictionary. Copyright © 1994, 2003 Biblesoft, Inc.
and International Bible Translators, Inc.)

SEASONS (moed) :
WITNESS/ Experienced back and forth as in repetition.
1349 Benner, Ancient Hebrew Lexicon of the Bible p.206

Ecclesiastes 3:1

3:1 To every thing there is a **season** , and a time to every
purpose under the heaven: KJV

Day 5
Living Creatures

A superficial assessment of Genesis 1:20 may lead one to misappropriate its true objectives by our insistence in identifying them as animals when they are in effect depicting **living** nephesh, or **living** creatures (as in Genesis 2:7; the living souls of men). The animation of creatures in Genesis 1:20 corresponds in kind to the comments of Jesus and the Apostles when they refer to covenant beings as being **quickened,** or given **new life** through salvation in Jesus Christ Eph.2:1, Col. 2:13. Jn.5:21.

The New Testament reference to covenant man as a new creature or creation should arrest our attention in this regard. The decay of the old life is passed away, and all things become new; that is, a new birth. The Hebraic usage of the word *nephesh* refers to all living organisms, including God himself (Jeremiah 6:8, 9:9). The Bible ascribes the word soul (nephesh) to God, humans, animals, fish, and also to that of fowls. The word nephesh does not always indicate a covenant entity; usually, the word living, new life, or simply it's setting in the text ultimately defines its designation.

The Immortal Soul

The word nephesh or soul is generally understood to be exclusively in the domain of humans, yet the Biblical record does not treat the word with such narrow parameters. This issue also exposes the fallacy of the "immortal soul" doctrine as propagated by most Christian systems of thought. The true doctrine of the nephesh poses a very difficult problem for those who believe that we are born with immortal souls. There is a teaching that says that animals and other living organisms cease to exist when they die because they do not possess an immortal soul, but according to the Hebrew, the term used is nephesh. If we insert the strict interpretation of the "immortal soul doctrine" into the Hebraic text, we must conclude the impossible that everlasting life resides in **all** life forms identified as a soul. There seems to be no reconciling of the fact that the scriptures teach that all men are mortal and are in desperate need of eternal life through Jesus Christ." (The soul that sinneth shall die." Ez. 18:20)

The English text shifts from the use of the term "soul" concerning Adam or man and switches to "creatures" when addressing animals. The confusion is due to creedal editing because the Hebrew text effectively contradicts a foundational tenant of universal Christendom. In essence, we do not *have* a soul; we *are* souls (nephesh).

"The distinction between the soul and body is something foreign to the Hebrew mentality, and death; therefore, is not regarded as the separation of these two elements. A live man is a living soul (nephesh) a dead man is a dead soul, a dead nephesh".
Roland de Vaux, OP. Ancient Israel its Life and Institutions p.56

When we are born a natural creature; we are born a dead spirit. To become a living soul, one needs to be born again of the water and the Spirit. Remember, Adam became a covenantal living soul. We are all born with the spirit of man; with a fallen shem, or character if you please. That character or shem experienced a transformation as we were born into the economy of the kingdom through the new birth experience. His character becomes our character through the process of forming and shaping depicted in the imagery of Genesis 2:7. The imagery of Genesis 2:7 fulfills itself in Revelation 3:12 as the name, breath, or character of God is written in those who have overcome by the blood of the Lamb and the word of their testimony. Through this new birth, we become living souls or living creatures.

Genesis 1:20

20 And God said, Let the waters bring forth abundantly the **moving creature (nephesh)** that hath life, and fowl that may fly above the earth in the open firmament of heaven KJV

Psalms 69:34

34 Let the heaven and earth praise him, the seas, and **every thing that moveth** therein. KJV

Genesis 1:21

Genesis 2:7

7 And the Lord God formed man *of* the dust of the ground, and breathed into his nostrils the breath of life; and man became **a living soul** (living nephesh). KJV

Genesis 1:21

21 And God created great whales, **and every living creature (soul ,nepesh)** that moveth, which the waters

brought forth abundantly, after their kind, and every winged fowl after his kind: and God saw that it was good. KJV

The creatures of Psalms 104:24-30 depict the provisions of God for his posterity. The provision ranges from the spiritual to the natural. The provision of "meat in due season" in this passage remains true to its hermeneutic pattern established throughout the Bible. Luke 12:42 aligns itself to this blueprint as Jesus assures the faithful of their reward "in due season." This dovetails with the concept of the seasons (moed) we referred to on day four of this chapter. Jesus was pointing to a designated time when the Church would collectively reap everlasting life; (the prophetic culmination of the harvest of souls).
'

Psalms 104:24-30

24 O Lord, how manifold are thy works! in wisdom hast thou made them all: the earth is full of thy riches.

25 So is this great and wide sea, wherein are things creeping innumerable, both small and great beasts.

26 There go the ships: there is that leviathan, whom thou hast made to play therein.

27 These wait all upon thee; that thou mayest give them their meat in due season.

28 That thou givest them they gather: thou openest thine hand, they are filled with good.

29 Thou hidest thy face, they are troubled: thou takest away their breath, they die, and return to their dust.

30 Thou sendest forth thy spirit, they are created: and thou renewest the face of the earth. KJV

Luke 12:42

42 And the Lord said, Who then is that faithful and wise steward, whom *his* lord shall make ruler over his household, to give *them their* **portion of meat in due season**? KJV

The *waters* are a general designation to humanity, out of which God divides and calls his people. The personification of "the waters" in Psalms 77:16-19 is remarkable as they assume the human attributes of awareness and fear. Similarly, the waters of humanity depict the same in Revelation 17:15, which serves as a faithful witness to the consistency of this relationship with these patterns.

Psalms 77:16-19

16 The waters saw thee, O God, **the waters saw thee; they were afraid: the depths also were troubled.**

Revelation 17:15

15 And he saith unto me, **The waters** which thou sawest, where the whore sitteth, **are peoples, and multitudes, and nations, and tongues**. KJV

Day Six
Beasts of the Earth

Please note that on day six, *the earth* brings forth the *living creatures*.

To be consistent with the covenantal usage of the word *earth*, its treatment in Genesis 1:24-27 produces a portrayal of generational birthing from covenant earth and is not of cosmic origins. The picture of cattle, fowl, fish, beasts, and creeping things lays the foundation for a prophetic form that utilized this precise imagery when referring to covenant entities throughout scripture. Furthermore, the biblical usage of the word *beast* constitutes the unregenerate or unconverted creature with the base urges and proclivities of the human condition. The use of this idiom becomes clear in Paul's struggle with unconverted men in Ephesus he called "beasts." 1 Corinthians 15:32

32 If after the manner of men **I have fought with beasts** at Ephesus, what advantageth it me, if the dead rise not? let us eat and drink; for to morrow we die.
KJV

Conversely, the regenerated status of the "creature" is usually preceded by the word "living."

Genesis 1:24-27

24 And God said, Let the earth bring forth the **living creature** (soul, nephesh) after his kind, cattle, and creeping thing, and beast of the earth after his kind: and it was so.

25 And God made the beast of the earth after his kind, and cattle after their kind, and everything that creepeth upon the earth after his kind: and God saw that it was good.

The "living creatures" of Ezekiel chapter one is a prime example of the covenantal usage to which we refer. The four faces of these creatures align themselves seamlessly with the four standards that represented the nation of Israel in the wilderness as they camped around the tabernacle of the LORD. The book of Revelation reinforces this imagery as the four "beasts" reproduced with the same four facial likenesses; however, they differ in appearance as having eyes within and without which is indicative of spiritual awareness. A depiction of the four and twenty elders replicates the imagery of the beasts with a multiple of 12's, which constitute a portrait of the entire Church. Both of these depictions essentially repeat the same message, a method utilized by Biblical writers throughout the sacred text.

Revelation 4:6-5:1

6 And before the throne *there was* a sea of glass like unto crystal: and in the midst of the throne, and round about the throne, *were* **four beasts full of eyes before and behind.**

7 And the first beast *was* like a **lion**, and the second beast like **a calf**, and the third beast had a **face as a man**, and the fourth beast *was* like a **flying eagle**.

8 And the four beasts had each of them six wings about *him*; and *they were* full of eyes within: and they rest not day and night, saying, Holy, holy, holy, Lord God Almighty, which was, and is, and is to come.

⁹ And when those beasts give glory and honour and thanks to him that sat on the throne, who liveth for ever and ever,

¹⁰ The four and twenty elders fall down before him that sat on the throne, and worship him that liveth for ever and ever, and cast their crowns before the throne, saying,

¹¹ Thou art worthy, O Lord, to receive glory and honour and power: for thou hast created all things, and for thy pleasure they are and were created. **KJV**

One of the most misappropriated scriptures in the history of Christendom is Isaiah 11:6- 9. Its prophetic portrait of covenant creatures living in harmony projects a time during which a period of peace with fraternal cooperation between animals and their prey. The unrelenting resistance to the covenantal implication of such scriptures is truly remarkable. The allegorical value of Noah and his ark generates the same imagery as Isaiah 11, as it promotes the same narratives. Once more, this demonstrates that the overarching account of the Bible is related to similar patterns and not ignored out of hand.

In effect, the endless infighting among scholars and professional ministry as concerning the various nuanced passages of scripture do not actuality verify the authenticity of the Bible as a whole. The story of the Bible is abundant with the type of patterns that relates its story in spite of the willful denial of the powers that be. Let us not forget the vision of unclean beasts to Peter on the housetop as the Lord reveals his plan to save the Gentiles through his preaching, reminding Peter not to call unclean what he has cleansed. It is this imagery that looms greater than the petty squabbling of those who guard cherished positions of the status quo. The replication of this particular imagery assigns the promise of covenantal reconciliation in spite of the base inclinations of the human condition. All of this attributed to the Prince of Peace, who, in spite of human resistance, brings us the victory through his name. Also, see Hosea 2:18-20

Isaiah 11:6-9

6 The wolf also shall dwell with the lamb, and the leopard shall lie down with the kid; and the calf and the young lion and the fatling together; and a little child shall lead them.

7 And the cow and the bear shall feed; their young ones shall lie down together: and the lion shall eat straw like the ox.

8 And the sucking child shall play on the hole of the asp, and the weaned child shall put his hand on the cockatrice' den.

9 They shall not hurt nor destroy in all my holy mountain: for the earth shall be full of the knowledge of the Lord, as the waters cover the sea. KJV

Hosea 2:18-20

18 And in that day will **I make a covenant** for them **with the beasts of the field, and with the fowls of heaven, and with the creeping things of the ground:** and I will break the bow and the sword and the battle out of the earth, and **will make them to lie down safely**

Chapter 5
The Seventh Day

(The last day or the day of Jesus Christ)

The last day in a series of seven days embodies the crowning work of God's Grace in the development of the covenant nation. The seventh day enters the sacred text at the beginning of the second chapter of Genesis. The shadow of this last day speaks of a ceasing of activity of the six days that preceded it. The English translations have uniformly translated the word **shabath** as "rest," but the word essentially means to cut or cease.... there is no connotation of the taking of rest or repose. God never needed to recuperate from creative activity; He is the eternal one that never sleeps (Ps. 23:3). Indeed, ceasing may invariably lead to a rest of sorts for a human, but the advent of its first mention Sabbath denotes the finality of the processes that preceded it (i.e., the cessation of work); thus, the subsequent entries of this word should be taken in the same vein if the context of the passage allows it.

The documented prophetic implications of the word Day is in the chapter entitled; "Light in a Dark Place." Our view of its function beginning in Genesis 1:5 and also its subsequent entries articulates the prophetic mode. Thus, expressions such as: the Day of the Lord, the Last Day, the Day of Jesus Christ, the Day of vengeance, in that day, the Day of his coming, the Day of Judgment, the Day of redemption, children of the day etc. all fit into the prophetic motif and should be employed as such.

The peculiarities of the expression "seventh day" and its affiliates usually fall into the same allegorical grouping. The depiction of a chronological Day is in verses that document a certain day in the lives of covenant people. The following passage (Genesis 2:1-4) expresses a prophetic view of the Seventh Day and qualifies as such with a supporting witness in the book of Hebrews Chapter 4. The writer of Hebrews strongly alludes to the mention of the cessation of God's work, as recorded in Hebrews 4:3-4. This declaration is stunning in that the writer is urging Hebrew Christians to cease from the works of the Mosaic Law. He gives them scriptural support to bolster the prophetic root of his argument by essentially referring to Genesis 2:1-4. **(For he spake in a certain place of the seventh *day* on this wise)**

The writer of Hebrews states that "the works were finished from the foundation of the (covenant) world." Hebrews 4:3 lends credence to his position that the ordinances of the Law were preordained to cease in their prophetic season. The words "foundation of the world" and "from the beginning" refers to the first few chapters of Genesis. These chapters serve as a prophetic springboard that initiates the events which follow the history of Israel and the first century Church.

Genesis 2:1-4

Thus the heavens and the earth were finished, and all the host of them.

2 And on the seventh day God ended his work which he had made; and he rested on the seventh day from all his work which he had made.

3 And God blessed **the seventh day**, and sanctified it: because that in it he had rested from all his work which God created and made.

4 These *are* the generations of the heavens and of the earth when they were created, in the day that the Lord God made the earth and the heavens, KJV

Hebrews 4:3-4

3 For we which have believed do enter into rest, as he said, As I have sworn in my wrath, if they shall enter into my rest: **although the works were finished from the foundation of the world.**

4 **For he spake in a certain place of the seventh** *day* **on this wise, And God did rest the seventh day** from all his works.KJV

Days one through six of Genesis One, all end with the expression, "The evening and the morning, were the ___ day." Curiously absent from the mention of the "*seventh day*" in Genesis 2: 1-4 is the omission of "evening and morning." The scribe did not unintentionally omit evening and morning. It was designed to direct our attention to the fact that six days of "work" had ceased and that the seventh day represented a different aspect of God's creation. In effect, the Seventh Day is loosed from the shadowy confinement of the preceding six days and stands as an open-ended expanse of prophetic time, which we term God's rest. There is a trove of references to this new dimension of Creation in New Testament writings. The ensuing teaching of the Apostles of the first-century documents a turning away from the **works** of the Mosaic economy to a "better covenant established on better promises." Thus, a transition of the covenants fulfilled in the New Testament Church through the prophetic underpinnings of Genesis chapters one and two.

Hebrews 8:6-7

6 But now hath he obtained a more excellent ministry, by how much also he is the mediator of **a better covenant**, which was established upon better promises.

7 For if that first *covenant* had been faultless, then should no place have been sought for the second. KJV

The Last Day

The Resurrection is alluded to as the "last day" in John 11:24. In our English vernacular, this would infer the last chronological day, but of what? Does it refer to the last chronological day of man's existence? Or do we see a prophetic context emerging? When we view similar entries into the sacred text, a more defined picture materializes.

John 11:24

24 Martha saith unto him, I know that he shall rise again in the resurrection at <u>the last day</u> KJV

Philippians 1:6

6 Being confident of this very thing, that he which hath begun a good work in you will perform it <u>until the day of Jesus Christ:</u> KJV

John 6:39-40

39 And this is the Father's will which hath sent me, that of all which he hath given me I should lose nothing, but should raise it up again at <u>the last day</u> .
40 And this is the will of him that sent me, that every one which seeth the Son, and believeth on him, may have everlasting life: and I will raise him up at <u>the last day.</u> KJV

The last day of the Feast of Tabernacles was a High Sabbath. There are seven High Sabbaths that frame the prophetic cycle of the Feasts of the Lord. Each High Sabbath signaled the future fulfillment of the ceasing from the ceremonial work commanded by Sinai. Leviticus 23:39 frames the yearly celebration of the Feast of Tabernacles with a High Sabbath on the 15th day and another on the 21st day, a seven-day feast.

Leviticus 23:39

39 Also in the fifteenth day of the **seventh month**, when ye have gathered in the fruit of the land, ye shall keep a feast unto the Lord seven days: on the first day shall be a Sabbath, and on the eighth day shall be a Sabbath. KJV

Jesus calls attention to an open-ended Pentecostal experience for the Church as it enters into this rest. The strategic placement of "rivers of living water" in the seventh month (The Feast of Tabernacles, the great Feast) may trouble those who try to make sense of the text; however, its placement points to a departure of the old patterns of work-worship to one of drawing close to God in a new and enduring way. The seventh feast in the seventh month fulfills the seventh prophetic day as foreshadowed by Genesis 2: 1-4.

John 7:37-38

37 In <u>the last day, that great day of the feast</u>, Jesus stood and cried, saying, If any man thirst, let him come unto me, and drink.

38 He that believeth on me, as the scripture hath said, out of his belly shall flow rivers of living water. KJV

We will have much more to say in Chapter 7 concerning the seventh day and its prophetic implications about the Feast of Tabernacles. Chapter 7 is entitled, "The Feasts of the Lord: The Blueprint for Prophetic Events."

Chapter 6

Let Us Make Man....

The primary prophetic objective of Genesis One can be summed up by the expression: "...Let us make man. All other patterns of scripture support this central theme of covenant relationship and converge upon this activity.

Genesis 1:26

26 And God said, **Let us make *man* in our image, after our likeness**....
and **let *them* have dominion** over the fish of the sea, and over the fowl of the air, and over the cattle, and over all the earth, and over every creeping thing that creepeth upon the earth. KJV

The high jacking of Genesis 1:26 no longer bears a resemblance to the narrative from which it originated. Conjecture, supposition, speculation, and outright guessing— have ruled the day when it comes to the interpretation of this beloved scripture. Some have speculated that the "us" indicated the very first revelation of a triune deity in declaring a work plan for creating humanity. Others have mused that the angels, in some mystical way, partook in the creative acts of YAHWEH. It is as if the honorable scribes have lost their way by disregarding an important rule of interpretation: if an expression does not fit the narrative, do not force its meaning until a Biblically appropriate path of interpretation presents itself. Whatever happened to the unpretentiously candid notion of saying, "I just don't know." As pastors, teachers, and scholars, why are we driven to produce answers to the obscure when, with time and patience, God ultimately illuminates the obscure with the aid of what is already known? These answers are available within plain sight:

"The first entry under "man" in Strong's concordance refers to this verse and supplies the number 120. Gesenius lexicon indicates that the Hebrew word אדם (transliterated Adam), and that its most basic, broadest, and most common meaning is a man or men in the sense of a particular specimen of the human race, or men in general." It has nothing to do with age or sex. Thus in the numerous contexts this word refers collectively to men, woman, and children. It is obvious from the whole context of Genesis 1:26-28 that the word (Adam) includes both male and female of the species. Thus the whole race, male and female is made is made in God's image and is to exercise dominion over the earth".

Publisher's introduction to Gesenius' Hebrew- Chaldee Lexicon of the Old Testament page vii

The following passage furnished further support of this view.:

Genesis 5:1-2

1.This *is* the book of the generations of Adam. *In the day that God created man (**Adam**),* in the likeness of God made he him;

2 Male and female created he them; and blessed them, *and called **their name Adam**, in the day when they were created.* KJV

6 And it came to pass, when men (Adam) began to multiply on the face of the earth, and daughters were born unto them,

2 That the sons of God saw the daughters of men that they *were* fair; and they took them wives of all which they chose. KJV

The creation of MAN as a corporate entity emerges from the prophetic text most lucidly as it fits when furnished with the support of passages like Psalms 102:18 and Isaiah 43: 5-9). Please note that the text (Gen.1:26-28) states **let *them* have dominion.** Thus, a tacit assumption exists among modern readers of the Bible is that Adam, the man was the subject of this creative activity. Gen.2:7, ("and God formed man (Adam) out of the dust of the ground) is also generally viewed as the creation of Adam, the individual. The creation of Eve illustrated in Genesis 2:21, drawn from the side of Adam. If we were to include Eve in the expression "let us make man" (Gen.1:26-28), then we would have corporate implications; we can't have it both ways. Either the reference to man in these scriptures refers to individuals, or they are a corporate designation indicating something much greater than the supposed narrative propagated today. There are several instances early on in Genesis that make overtures to a corporate creation that became a foundational tenet for the balance of holy writ. The Bible consistently guides the reader on the path of the future when it discusses the birthing of the covenant nation.

Psalms 102:18

18 Let this be written for a future generation,
that a people not yet created(*bara*) may praise the Lord:
NIV

 In Isaiah 43:5-9 the statements not only address the future generations of covenant life but also the past.

Isa 43:5-9

5 Fear not: for I am with thee: **I will bring thy seed** from the east, and gather thee from the west;

6 I will say to the north, Give up; and to the south, Keep not back: bring my sons from far, and my daughters from the ends of the earth;

7 *Even every one that is called by my name: for I **have created (bara) him for my glory, I have formed him; yea, I have made him.***

8 Bring forth the blind people that have eyes, and the deaf that have ears.

9 Let all the nations be gathered together, and let the people be assembled: who among them can declare this,
and shew us former things? let them bring forth their witnesses, that they may be justified: or let them hear, and say, It is truth. KJV

The Corporate Motif: The Temple

The various prophetic applications of the word "day" essentially find their roots in the creation week of Genesis One. All to be born in the kingdom covenant corporately find themselves in this narrative. Genesis One signified the past, present, and future birth of man's covenant existence. The foundation of this first temple was laid with the creation of Adam in the Garden of Eden and continued through to the coming of Christ into his eternal Sabbath. The inception of a temple motif originated in the Garden of Eden, and it is the first portrayal of the cohabitation of God and Man. John Walton touched on this subject as he viewed the purpose of Genesis One similarly.

"We have suggested that the seven days are not given as a period of time over which the material cosmos came into existence, but the period of time devoted to the inauguration of functions of the cosmic temple"... **John Walton. The Lost World of Genesis One, p.91**

Although disqualified from the intimacy of the Garden, Adam inadvertently became the high priest of a work-based system established in the third chapter of Genesis. The system required three basic ingredients: a temple, a high priest, and a sacrificial system. This fixed order demonstrated the consequences of sin and judgment that was never intended to rehabilitate either Adam or his descendants. The more sin flourished, the more elaborate and detailed its ceremonial maneuverings articulated. In due course, the system established in Genesis Chapter 3 was eventually synthesized and codified on Mount Sinai. In its allusion to creation, judgment, and the Law, the reference of early Genesis as "the foundation of the world." (i.e., the foundation of the covenant world). We will study this aspect of our treatise in the chapter entitled, "The Foundation of the World."

Mount Sinai and Genesis One

Another place where we view this cohabitation of God and man through their related imagery is on
Mount Sinai. In effect, The Tabernacle of Moses presents a recreation of the Genesis motif within a three-dimensional format. It is called the "Tent of Meeting." The correlation between these two "creation" motifs are striking.

"Both Tabernacle and cosmos come to exist through a six fold creative act culmination in a seventh act of rest. Six times we read, "The Lord said unto Moses; Exodus 25:1, 30:11, 17, 22, 34, 31:1 which parallels six creative words of Genesis 1: "And God said...vvs.3, 6, 9, 14, 20, and 22. These six creative acts are followed by the seventh, "The Lord said unto Moses in Exodus 30:12which introduced the Sabbath command. This suggests to many readers past and present that building the Tabernacle is a microcosm, the recreation of the cosmos on a smaller scale.
Jon D. Levenson, Creation and the Persistence of Evil: The Jewish Drama of Divine Omnipotence. 1988 pp.53- 127

As we begin to view the first five chapters of Genesis with this covenantal perspective, we observe the corporate body personified in Adam as the Law which exercised dominion over covenant man (beasts, fish, fowl of the air, etc.) until the consummation of the Body (i.e., till the Sabbath of the seventh prophetic day). As we have stated earlier, the Garden of Eden holds the first suggestion of the corporate / temple motif in chapter one and verse 26. It was the Garden where God initially communed with Adam in the ruash, breath, or Spirit of the day. They communed amid the trees of the garden of God, and Adam became the covenant world's first high priest. The allusion to this principle referred to the dispossession of Israel in its 70-year exile and represented to in the following verse:

Lamentations 2:6

6 And He shaketh **as a garden His tabernacle**, He hath destroyed His **appointed place**, Jehovah hath forgotten in Zion the appointed time and sabbath, And despiseth, in the indignation of His anger, king and priest. YLT

Covenant Births

It was in Genesis 1:26 that the corporate body (temple) was first introduced in allegory when it unveiled the eternal purpose of the passage. The basis upon which we view the statements of Genesis 1:26 as a corporate creation of man is simply by the event and that the text clearly defines them as such. The words "let *them* have dominion..." infer that the "*man*" created is no more than a personification alluding to covenant people. It is not referring to the historical figures we know as Adam and Eve. The corporate nature of the expression "let us make man" also lends itself to the conclusion that the ministry of covenantal births is a corporate endeavor illustrated in the Bible as Adam and Eve, and later inversely in scripture as the Bride and the Bridegroom. Chapter 2 of Genesis serves as a summation of the creation account of Genesis One and Two. It begins with a bewildering statement in verse one.

Genesis 2:1-4
2:1 Thus the heavens and the earth were finished, and all the host of them.

This statement denotes the seven days of creation in a consummated state of completion. The curious thing about the verse is that the word host does not refer solely to Adam and Eve. The word is defined primarily as a mass of persons.

HOST:OT:6635 tsaba' (tsaw-baw'); OT:6633; a mass of persons (or figuratively, things), especially reg. organized for war (an army); by implication, a campaign, literally or figuratively
(Biblesoft's New Exhaustive Strong's Numbers and Concordance.

The Mechanical Translation of Genesis says it this way:

"And the sky and the land and *** all of their armies*** were finished".
page 20 Jeff Benner

The Old Testament employs the word host (tsaba) 486 times specifically about the armies of Israel (or to

Israel as bodies politick). This fact stands defiantly against the notion which most assert that the narrative of Genesis One must be a story of the creation of two human beings amid a universal cosmological event.

This apparent obstruction to the official cosmological narrative does not stand alone in the earlier chapters of Genesis. Additional evidence emerges seemingly out of every quarter if one pays the slightest attention to the detail of the texts. Verse 4 reinforces this inference to a mass of covenant beings by its statement that these "births" or generations were the product of Genesis One. Genesis One does not conspicuously announce the mass births alluded to in Genesis 2 but stated in highly figurative statements written within the context of its six creative days. The portrayal of a corporate six-day creation motif in scripture as the "day" of the creation of man. Evidently, Genesis 2:1-4 is not strictly referring to the seventh day because the usage of the term "day" definitely has prophetic implications with its suggestion of massive births created in the six previous days of Genesis One.

Genesis 2:3-4

3 And God blesseth the seventh day, and sanctifieth it, for in it He hath ceased from all His work which God had prepared for making.

4 These [are] births of the heavens and of the earth in their being prepared, in the day of Jehovah God's making earth and heavens; YLT

It is clear that Isaiah 41:4 has its counterpart in Gen.2:3-4

Isaiah 41:4

4 Who has done this and carried it through, *forth calling the generations from the beginning*? I, the Lord — with the first of them and with the last — I am he." NIV

The following passages replicate a similar sentiment.

Isaiah 46:10

10 I make known the end from the beginning, from ancient times, what is still to come. I say: My purpose will stand, and I will do all that I please.
NIV

Ps 102:18

18 This will be written for the generation to come;
That a people yet to be created may praise the Lord.
NASB

One of the best illustrations in defending our position is in Genesis 5:1-2. It serves as the first genealogy into the sacred text. The genealogy spans ten covenantal generations from Adam to Noah, but special attention should draw to the expression "in the *day that God created man.*" The reference to a day of creation comprised of ten covenantal generations would appear contradictory if interpreted in the typical literal motif ascribed to the first chapter of Genesis. The passage chronicles the historical generations of these men, but it is done so in a prophetic mode with the usage of the word DAY. This further substantiates our contention that the

191

usage of the word *day* in Genesis chapters 1-5 are not a twenty-four-hour interval but are indeed prophetic. Verse two decisively nails the corporate motif by stating that God blessed and collectively referred to our covenant ancestors as 'Adam." Please note the expression, "Male and female created he them"... this did not solely refer to "Adam and Eve" because the context in which this was written deliberately refers to a corporate organism. The referral to Genesis 1:26 is identifiable when one recognizes the nature of both texts as they conjoin in Biblical intent.

Genesis 5:1-2
5:1 This is the book of the generations of Adam. *In the day that God created man,* in the likeness of God made he him;

2 Male and female created he them; and blessed them, *and called their name Adam,* **in the day** *when they were created.*

Genesis 5:1-2
1. This is the scroll of the birthings of the human in the day Elohim fattened the human in the likeness of Elohim he did him.
2. Male and female he fattened them and he respected them, and he called them out their title human in the day he fattened them.
Mechanical Translation of the Book of Genesis, J.Benner

Please note the Hebrew parallelism that frames the principal actor of the text (Is.66:8-9) as it illustrates terms related to covenant people such as (Earth, Nation, Zion). These are but a few of the many references identifying covenant people as a corporate entity.

Isaiah 66:8-9

8 Who hath heard such a thing? who hath seen such things? Shall:

- **the earth** be made to bring forth **in one day**? or
- shall **a nation** be born at once? For as soon as
- **Zion** travailed, she brought forth her children.

9 Shall I bring to the birth, and not cause to bring forth? saith the Lord: shall I cause to bring forth, and shut the womb? saith thy God. KJV

Jerusalem our Mother

The development of the husband-wife -children scenario established in prophetic writing as the Biblical drama between the creator and his children unfolds. Genesis 1:26 initiated that pattern with the expression, "let us make man." The cooperation between God and man in covenantal intimacy alluded to in Galatians 4:25-27 in stating that *above Jerusalem is called the "mother of us all."* Jerusalem is the personification of new covenant believers as opposed to the *"Jerusalem that now is,"* which embodied in Hagar, the Law, and all its constituents. In essence, the passage portrays two mothers, two classifications of children, and two covenants. This style of covenantal language undoubtedly traces its roots to Genesis 1:26. The genealogical presentation in the earliest parts of Genesis 1, 2, 4, and 5 are relating the same covenantal narrative. That narrative is not comprised of a cosmological, scientific motif as concerning the founding of the universe but is only formulated to document covenantal paternity between the Father and his creation.

Galatians 4:25-27

25 for this Hagar is mount Sinai in Arabia, and doth correspond to the Jerusalem that _now [is]_, and is in servitude with her children,

26 and the Jerusalem _above_ is the free-woman, _which is mother of us all,_

27 for it hath been written, 'Rejoice, O barren, who art not bearing; break forth and cry, thou who art not travailing, because many [are] the children of the desolate — more than of her having the husband.' YLT

The Harlot Bride

Hosea delineated the husband and wife scenario of the covenantal relationship in very graphic detail. Note the handling of the term "day" in the passage. Consistent with prophetic convention, the word _day_ refers to the creation or birth of covenantal relationship we have discovered in the earlier portions of Genesis; however, it is also perpetuated throughout covenantal history and sustained into the unforeseen future. The imagery in Hosea places the prophet in the stead of "God the husband," and Gomer, the adulteress wife, is typified as Israel. It is very important to recognize the development of this prophetic drama, which unfolds in the holy script. It is as if God is saying to Hosea, I am married to an adulteress; now you must marry one to understand my plight. The names of Hosea's children are a prophetic testimonial of Israel's state of affairs. God pronounced a judgment of dispersion of the Northern Kingdom by the naming of Hosea's children. On the other hand, God promised restoration to both Israel and Judah in a pledge of eternal love and devotion.

Hosea 2:2-5

2 Plead with your mother, plead: for she is not my wife, neither am I her husband: let her, therefore, put away her whoredoms out of her sight, and her adulteries from between her breasts;

3 Lest I strip her naked, and set her *as in the **day** that she was born*, and make her as a wilderness, and set her like a dry land, and slay her with thirst.

4 And I will not have mercy upon her children; for they be the children of whoredoms. KJV

The promise of kingdom restoration (see below) made to Israel by Hosea through a new covenant is eerily reminiscent of the language of Genesis One. We believe that it was written with the intent of reemphasizing the covenantal imagery and truths by which Israel was well acquainted. Why would Hosea refer to cosmology or a scientific event when promising a restored kingdom to Israel? It does not make any sense unless the symbolic nature of the passage in Genesis One indeed characterized the kingdom in its original creative state. We believe that Israel was well acquainted with that sort of language.

Verse 18 also uses the word day in the prophetic genre. Thus, we have the usage of the word day in verse three with the birth of the old covenant and the usage of the word day in a future covenant. All references to the word *day*, in the posture of true prophetic expression, have their origins articulated in the seven days of creation. Our natural inclination to look back historically to a seven- day cosmological event has only served to misinform us. Conversely, the seven- day creation motif has always directed us into the future for its fulfillment. Our vital task is to remind students that in Biblical times, the prophetic expressions attributed to the word *day* owed its legitimacy to the statements made in the first chapter of Genesis.

Hosea 2:18-23

18 *And in that day will I make a covenant for them with the beasts of the field, and with the fowls of heaven, and with the creeping things of the ground*: and I will break the bow and the sword and the battle out of the earth, and will make them to lie down safely.

19 And I will *betroth* thee unto me for ever; yea, I will betroth thee unto me in righteousness, and in judgment, and in lovingkindness, and in mercies.
20 I will even betroth thee unto me in faithfulness: and thou shalt know the Lord.
21 And it shall come to pass *in that day*, I will hear, saith the Lord, I will hear the heavens, and they shall hear the earth;
22 And the earth shall hear the corn, and the wine, and the oil; and they shall hear Jezreel.

23 And I will sow her unto me in the earth; and I will have mercy upon her that had not obtained mercy; and I will say to them which were not my people, Thou art my people; and they shall say, Thou art my God. KJV

The Bride and the Bridegroom

Isaiah 62:4-5

4 Thou shalt no more be termed Forsaken; neither shall thy land any more be termed Desolate: but thou shalt be called Hephzi-bah, and thy land Beulah: for the Lord delighteth in thee, and thy land shall be married.

5 For as a young man marrieth a virgin, so shall thy sons marry thee: and as the bridegroom rejoiceth over the bride, so shall thy God rejoice over thee.KJV

Isaiah 66:7-12

7 Before she travailed, she brought forth; before her pain came, she was delivered of a man child.

8 Who hath heard such a thing? who hath seen such things? Shall the earth be made to bring forth in one day? or shall a nation be born at once? for as soon as Zion travailed, she brought forth her children.
9 Shall I bring to the birth, and not cause to bring forth? saith the Lord: shall I cause to bring forth, and shut the womb? saith thy God.

10 Rejoice ye with Jerusalem, and be glad with her, all ye that love her: rejoice for joy with her, all ye that mourn for her:

11 That ye may suck, and be satisfied with the breasts of her consolations; that ye may milk out, and be delighted with the abundance of her glory.

12 For thus saith the Lord, Behold, I will extend peace to her like a river, and the glory of the Gentiles like a flowing stream: then shall ye suck, ye shall be borne upon her sides, and be dandled upon her knees.
KJV

The prophetic drama portrays a future betrothal that gradually developed in stature and is vividly expressed in the scriptural imagery recorded in the Psalms, Song of Solomon, Hosea, Joel, Jeremiah, as well as the words of Jesus Christ, John the Baptist, and the Apostles.

Psalms 19:4-6

4 Their line is gone out through all the earth, and their words to the end of the world. In them hath he set a tabernacle for the sun,

5 Which is as a bridegroom coming out of his chamber, and rejoiceth as a strong man to run a race

6 His going forth is from the end of the heaven, and his circuit unto the ends of it: and there is nothing hid from the heat thereof. KJV

Joel 2:16

16 Gather the people, sanctify the congregation, assemble the elders, gather the children, and those that suck the breasts: let the bridegroom go forth of his chamber, and the bride out of her closet KJV

Covenant Dominion (the image of God)

One of the covenantal functions of God's creation is the exercise of kingdom dominion, i.e., the impartation of kingdom authority stated in Genesis 1:26. In its literal rendering, the following passage referring to authority over fish, birds, and cattle seems to be preposterously irrelevant unless viewed in a covenantal sense. The allusion to these living creatures in prophecy is pervasive throughout the Bible and has no bearing on biological forms of life.

Genesis 1:26

26 And God said, Let us make man in our image, after our likeness: and *let them have dominion over the fish of the sea, and over the fowl of the air, and over the cattle, and over all the earth, and over every creeping thing that creepeth upon the earth.* KJV

The woman (city) referred to in Revelation 17 is Jerusalem, the seat of kingdom authority over all its subjects. Israel did not rule over Rome or any other nation in the time of its writing. Note the present tense usage for the word *reigneth*. John identified this system as existing in his time. Is this "Harlot" reigning over the kings of the whole planet, or does her dominion limit itself to the kings of the covenant realm? Here again, we see the universal usage of the word "earth" misappropriated because of a dogma of universalism. For years the evangelical movement has portrayed the Catholic Church as this wicked universal system. The whole matter could be laid at rest by reading the text in its proper chronological setting; that is, in the time of John. The speculations of modern Bible teachers identify the woman in this passage as the Catholic Church, which was not in existence at the time of John's writing.

Revelation 17:18

18 And the woman which thou sawest is that great city, which *reigneth over the kings of the earth. KJV*

Revelation 5:9-10

9 And they sung a new song, saying, Thou art worthy to take the book, and to open the seals thereof: for thou wast slain, and hast redeemed us to God by thy blood out of every kindred, and tongue, and people, and nation;

10 And hast made us unto our God kings and priests: and we shall reign on the earth. KJV

The following admonition to kings seems to be out of place, knowing David himself wrote this early psalm. I believe that this statement was an emblematic referral to Israel, a nation of kings. Psalms 2:10

*10 Be wise now therefore, O **ye kings** : be instructed, ye judges of the earth. KJV*

Jacob Understood Genesis 1:14

A curious event occurred during the life of Jacob and his son Joseph. Joseph related a dream that he had concerning the sun, moon, and the stars. Those of us that are familiar with the story know that the sun, moon, and the stars prostrated themselves before Joseph. Jacob immediately understood the symbolic nature of Joseph's dream and attributed the luminaries to his own family. There is a question we should ask ourselves: how did this Bedouin of ancient times understand the significance of that dream? What external point of reference could he have accessed to derive such a conclusion?. The 14th verse of Genesis One was a part of the oral tradition of their history passed down from generation to generation. We believe that this oral history originated from the lips of his forefathers. Jacob's view of his covenantal pedigree was not cosmological. I wonder who would dare argue with the patriarch in regarding his perception of Joseph's dream. If Jacob held a literal view of his son's dream, he would have dismissed the dream as pure fantasy and his son a raving lunatic. This provides more proof that the ancients did not view creation as a mere cosmology but as an intimate narrative of the covenantal relationship between themselves and God.

An additional prophetic counterpart of Genesis 1:14-18 is Revelation 22:4-5. This scripture illustrates the restoration of man into the presence of God (we see his face), and the character of our God (his name) is in our will (our foreheads). The need for the lampstand of the sanctuary and the perpetuation of the prophetic convocations of Genesis 1:14-18 (the sun) outlive their usefulness because they come into fulfillment through the light of the new temple, the body of Christ.

Revelation 22:4-5

4 and they shall see His face, and His name [is] upon their foreheads,

5 and **night shall not be there**, and they have no need of a lamp and light of a sun, because the Lord God doth give them light, and they shall reign — to the ages of the ages. YLT

Further evidence of this pattern found in Revelation 12:1. If consistency is maintained, its first mention in Genesis One and Jacob's perception of its underpinnings are fairly easy to ascertain. Its elements define the identity of this mysterious woman.

Revelation 12:1-4

12:1 And there appeared a great wonder in heaven; **a woman clothed with the sun, and the moon under her feet, and upon her head a crown of twelve stars:**

2 And **she being with child cried, travailing in birth**, and pained to be delivered.

3 And there appeared another wonder in heaven; and behold a great red dragon, having seven heads and ten horns, and seven crowns upon his heads.

4 And his tail drew the third part of the stars of heaven, and did cast them to the earth: and the dragon stood before the woman which was ready to be delivered, for to devour her child as soon as it was born. KJV

Chapter 7
The Feasts of Israel: The Pattern of Prophetic Events

Genesis One and the Feasts of Israel are unquestionably related as they work together to establish a prophetic foundation for the balance of holy writ. How do we justifiably sustain this assertion, especially regarding the Feasts of Israel? Genesis One confirms its relationship with the Feasts of Israel through its a seven- day template whereby subsequent multiples of days, weeks, months, and years emerge to create a sort of predictive agricultural time clock that serves to predict future events for the redemption of man. Primary evidence of this premise occurs at Mount Sinai as its Seven Feast pattern developed upon the foundation of the seven day week:

Exodus 23:12

12 Six days thou shalt do thy work, and on the seventh day thou shalt rest: that thine ox and thine ass may rest, and the son of thy handmaid, and the stranger, may be refreshed.

14 Three times thou shalt keep a feast unto me in the year.

15 Thou shalt keep the feast of unleavened bread: (thou shalt eat unleavened bread seven days, as I commanded thee, in the time appointed of the month Abib; for in it thou camest out from Egypt: and none shall appear before me empty:)

16 And the feast of harvest, the firstfruits of thy labours, which thou hast sown in the field: and the feast of ingathering, *which is* in the end of the year, when thou hast gathered in thy labours out of the field.

17 Three times in the year all thy males shall appear before the Lord God.

The agricultural patterns engendered within the Feasts are readily identifiable throughout the writings of the prophets, notably in the teachings of our Lord. The gathering of the wheat, barley, grapes, and the like have long been understood to foreshadow the appointed ingathering of covenant people for their salvation and redemption.

Leviticus 23:3-44 restated the directives regarding these Feasts but ventures into much greater detail than that of Exodus 23. Numbers chapters 28-29 and Deuteronomy chapter 16 also record various aspects of the Feasts. It's a system founded upon a multiple of sevens, and each Feast seemingly framed with what the Bible defines as "High Sabbaths" or a "High Day."(There are seven of these high Sabbaths within this seven-month festive cycle).

The Jews celebrated within seven months during the religious year, which begins with the Spring Barley Harvest. On the tenth day of the first month, a lamb is selected and inspected for flaws or imperfections. The fourteenth day (two sets of sevens) is designated for the slaying of the Passover Lamb, thus foreshadowing the death of Jesus Christ as its fulfillment. At sundown (the 15th), A High Sabbath commences (After Christ's crucifixion) that initiates a seven- day period called the Feast of Unleavened Bread. At the end of that seven- day period they had the observance of another High Sabbath. Amid these seven days (the third day), we have the Feast of First Fruits. Jesus fulfilled that shadow with his resurrection. He was the First Fruits of them that slept (1 Corinthians 15:20). Seven weeks and a High Sabbath (49+1) later focus on the wheat harvest commonly called the Feast of Pentecost, or the Feast of Weeks. This also commemorated the birth of Israel at Mount Sinai, as it foreshadows its fulfillment in the initial pages of Acts as the birthday of the Church. Four months afterward, the great harvest alluded to by Jesus in John 4:5 initiated by the final three Feasts, which comprise the Feast of Trumpets, Atonement, and Tabernacles. This passage forthrightly reveals the imagery of the Feasts' agricultural motif as the harvest of souls.

John 4:35

35 Say not ye, There are yet four months, and *then* cometh harvest? behold, I say unto you, Lift up your eyes, and look on the fields; for they are white already to harvest. KJV

The first day (A High Sabbath) of the seventh month initiates this Sabbatical month as the Feast of Trumpets, which proclaims the ingathering of the last harvest. On the tenth day (A High Sabbath) of the month, the Feast of Atonement is celebrated for the atonement for sin for the nation of Israel. On the Fifteenth day of the month (A High Sabbath), the last and final feast (Tabernacles) begins and celebrated for seven days. The Seventh-day of this feast is also a High Sabbath and thus concludes the agricultural cycle of the Festive year.

The final week of sevens illustrated in the Feasts of

Israel is the Feast of Tabernacles. It falls in the seventh and final month of the religious cycle. The finality of its appearance in the prophetic pattern should arrest our attention. The seventh and concluding month referred to as the sabbatical month. The seventh day of the creation week finds its ultimate fulfillment in The Feast of Tabernacles for seven days in length. The first (15th) and last (21st) day of the Feast are also High Sabbaths. The significance of these Feasts should not be dismissed or hastily overlooked because all of the six preceding Feasts essentially enter into this seventh and final Feast of rest. We believe that the purposes of prophetic fulfillment expressed with this preoccupation of Sabbatical destinations reflected in the solemn pledge by Christ to bring his beloved followers into his rest.

Matthew 11:28

¶ **28** Come unto me, all ye that labour and are heavy laden, and I will give you rest. KJV

Take a Closer Look

When an event in the Bible makes a particular notation as to a month and day, it is beckoning the reader for a closer examination of its content. For example, Noah's ark **rested** on Mount Ararat on the **seventeenth day in the seventh month** (Gen. 8:4) after the tribulation of a catastrophic flood. Can anyone say that this chronological designation is insignificant, being that the ark **rested** amid the feast of Tabernacles? (Duration of the feast is the 15th to the 21st)

The correlation made by Jesus and the Apostles to aspects of the Noachian flood is noteworthy. The parallels drawn by them as concerning the tribulation of the Jewish economy and the Flood are purposely to illustrate the totality of its devastation. In both cases, those who survived the desolation of their era entered into a time of peace and renewal. On the one hand, Noah inherits a new world, and the Church, a new age. This is why greater scrutiny of the events adjoining the dedication of Solomon's Temple. Its internal narration should bear an exhaustive examination to glean a fullness of understanding of such an important topic.

The Dedication of the Temple

Genesis One is a statement of prophecy that prefigures the history of man's struggle to keep the Law of God unto the entering of Gods' eternal Temple. This prophetic type reenacted in the week of days allotted for the dedication of the temple of Solomon. The end of the old covenant with its system of works (six days) surrenders itself to the peace of its eternal Sabbath (the seventh day).

The Temple of Solomon fits an Old Testament type fulfilled as the New Testament Church in its future majesty and glory. It is where the ancient system of Old Testament works comes to its final resting place in the New. 2 Chronicles 5:2-9 vividly illustrates where the Ark is recorded to be in transition from the Tabernacle of David (where it resided for 40 years) to the Temple of Solomon. The pomp and ceremony depicted in the following passage, prophetically illustrate its final journey to rest. Note that the utilization of staves used in locomotion for hundreds of years was then permanently removed, thus ending the long journey from without the gates of Eden, now into heaven itself.

2 Chronicles 5:2-9

2 Then Solomon assembled the elders of Israel, and all the heads of the tribes, the chief of the fathers of the children of Israel, unto Jerusalem, to bring up the ark of the covenant of the Lord out of the city of David, which is Zion.

3 Wherefore all the men of Israel assembled themselves unto the king in **the feast which was in the seventh month**

4 And all the elders of Israel came; and the Levites took up the ark.

5 And they brought up the ark, and the tabernacle of the congregation, and all the holy vessels that were in the tabernacle, these did the priests and the Levites bring up.

6 Also king Solomon, and all the congregation of Israel that were assembled unto him before the ark, sacrificed sheep and oxen, which could not be told nor numbered for multitude.

7 And the priests brought in the ark of the covenant of the Lord unto his place, to the oracle of the house, into the most holy place, even under the wings of the cherubims:

8 For the cherubims spread forth their wings over the place of the ark, and the cherubims covered the ark and the staves thereof above.

9 And **they drew out the staves of the ark** that the ends of the staves were seen from the ark before the oracle; but they were not seen without. **And there it is unto this day.** KJV

 2 Chronicles 7:8-9

8 Also at the same time Solomon kept the **feast seven days**, and all Israel with him, a very great congregation, from the entering in of Hamath unto the river of Egypt.

9 And in the eighth day they made a solemn assembly: **for they kept the dedication of the altar seven days, and the feast seven days.** KJV

10 And on the three and twentieth day of the seventh month he sent the people away into their tents, glad and merry in heart for the goodness that the Lord had shewed unto David, and to Solomon, and to Israel his people. KJV

The end of this prophetic journey ushered in the commencement of eternal Sabbatical rest for the Church, the tabernacle, or body of Jesus Christ. That body initiated its development prophetically in Adam and realized its completion in Christ. The following passage marks the end of the agricultural feasts with its many types. The King James Version inadvertently obscured its intent; therefore, we have here surveyed its veiled implications with the original Hebrew and additional versions of the Bible for clarity. Note that the prophetic passage not only declares an end of the seasons (or feasts) but more importantly, the imagery develops resolutely into a New

Testament fulfillment through the expression **"that living waters shall go out from Jerusalem."**

 Special note: Jesus predicted that "Repentance and remission of sins should be preached in his name beginning at Jerusalem." Thus the prophetic timetable of the Holy Ghost outpouring had chronological and geographical markers.

On that day, there shall be no more seasons.

Seasons or convocations (feasts) to cease forever

Zechariah 14:6-8

6 And it shall come to pass in that day, that the light shall not be **clear, nor dark:**

7 But it shall be one day which shall be known to the Lord, not day, nor night: but it shall come to pass, that at evening time it shall be light.

8 And it shall be in that day, **that living waters shall go out from Jerusalem;** half of them toward the former sea, and half of them toward the hinder sea: in summer and in winter shall it be. KJV

DARK (Parent root 413) :The sun speaks....Seasons As the sun travels through the sky it marks the times and seasons (Genesis 1:14)

CLEAR: Parent root 416 : Gather the men....meeting . The men often came together during the cool of the day to discuss news of the camp. A calling for assembly. <small>Jeff A.bennerAncient Hebrew Language and Alphabet page 172</small>

The moed ceases and comes into its REST.

The cessation of light, darkness, day, and night in prophetic context compels its narrative to be viewed uniquely in the light of Genesis One. The six days of Genesis One with its evenings and mornings cease with the advent of the seventh day, where there is no more mention of evening or morning. In essence, the Sabbath is not defined with evening and morning as the previous six days were, and for a good reason. The prophetic time clock ceases with the introduction of the seventh day into the sacred text as "the evening and the morning" is seemingly redacted from the Genesis account.

Although Hosea 2:10-11 graphically expresses the sin of Israel and threatens judgment through the cessation of its Sabbaths and solemn feasts, God does not stop there. In verses 14-19, He makes a provision of deliverance through a new covenant after her judgment in the wilderness. He "speaks" to her through the word and ultimately betroths her in a new holy union forever. Please note that God makes this covenant with "the beasts of the field and with the fowls of heaven, and *with* the creeping things of the ground." This serves as a proof text for the covenant creatures (people) depicted in Days 5 and 6. The picture generated by these "beasts" lying down alludes to the imaginary notions of the so-called millennium represented by Is.11: 6-7 as it perpetuates the Sabbatical rest assured to the Church through the preaching of Christ.

Hosea 2:10-11

10 And now will I discover her lewdness in the sight of her lovers, and none shall deliver her out of mine hand.

11 I will also cause all her mirth to cease, her feast days, her new moons, and her sabbaths, and all her solemn feasts.KJV

Hosea 2:14-19

14 Therefore, behold, I will allure her, and bring her into the wilderness, and speak comfortably unto her.

15 And I will give her her vineyards from thence, and the valley of Achor for a door of hope: and she shall sing there, as in the days of her youth, and as in the day when she came up out of the land of Egypt.

16 And it shall be at that day, saith the Lord, *that* thou shalt call me Ishi; and shalt call me no more Baali.

17 For I will take away the names of Baalim out of her mouth, and they shall no more be remembered by their name.

18 And in that day **will I make a covenant for them with the beasts of the field, and with the fowls of heaven, and *with* the creeping things of the ground: and I will break the bow and the sword and the battle out of the earth, and will make them to lie down (*to rest*) safely.**

19 And I will betroth thee unto me for ever; yea, I will betroth thee unto me in righteousness, and in

judgment, and in lovingkindness, and in mercies.

Isaiah 11:6-7

6 The wolf also shall dwell with the lamb, and the leopard shall lie down with the kid; and the calf and the young lion and the fatling together, and a little child shall lead them.

7 And the cow and the bear shall feed; their young ones **shall lie down together**: and the lion shall eat straw like the ox. KJV

Evening and morning is no more!

Zechariah 14:6-7

6 On that day there will be no light, no cold or frost. 7 It will be a unique day, without daytime or nighttime

— a day known to the Lord. When evening comes, there will be light. NIV

Zechariah 14:6
6 When that time comes, there will no longer be cold or frost, TEV
Zechariah 14:6

6 In that day there will be no light; the luminaries will dwindle NASU

Zechariah 14:6

6 And it shall come to pass in that day, that there shall not be light; the bright ones shall withdraw themselves ASV

Zechariah 14:6

6 And it shall come to pass in that day that there shall not be light; the glorious and bright ones [the heavenly bodies] shall be darkened. AMP

Zechariah 14:6

6 The sun and moon and stars will no longer shine, TLB

Zechariah 14:6

6 On that day the sources of light will no longer shine

Chapter 8
The Foundation of the World

The rise and fall of Adam inadvertently led to the institution of the ceremonial approach to God. This period in Biblical history referred to many times as *"the foundation of the world.* The term "foundation of the world" is a statement viewed through the prism of man's covenantal ancestry. Unfortunately, the classic use of the term applied in a universal/ cosmic sense as opposed to its strictly defined covenantal narrative. The Bible alternately uses the term "foundation of the earth." Numerous times the terms "earth" and "world" are used reciprocally as are the terms "kingdom of God" and "kingdom of heaven." As we have noted earlier, those terms (earth and world) are utilized to draw attention to the covenantal earth or world if you please. There is a contingent among those within the ranks of the fulfilled prophecy movement who feel the terminology "foundation of the world" refers only to the codification of the Law on Mount Sinai, but as we shall see, scriptural evidence yields a different conclusion. A good example of this confused perception stems from their view of Hebrews 1:10-12. The passage is understood by both partial and full preterists to signify the transition of the covenants (we heartily agree with that conclusion). The point of contention nevertheless arises when one inquires as to the significance of verse 10. They vigorously deny the destruction of the cosmos in that passage, and yet the apparent reference to the "foundation of the world" and its creation inspires a sort of dyslexic response from them because of a strict preoccupation with a cosmological approach to creation. Instead, they disregard the apparent covenantal relationship between verse 10 (In the beginning...) and its first mention in Genesis 1:1.

Hebrews 1:10-12

10 And, Thou, Lord, **in the beginning** hast laid the foundation of the earth; and the heavens are the works of thine hands:

11 They shall perish; but thou remainest; and they all **shall wax old** as doth a garment;

12 And as a vesture shalt thou fold them up, and *they shall be changed:* but thou art the same, and thy years shall not fail. KJV

Hebrews 8:13 is a confirmation of a covenant in transition addressed in Hebrews 1:10-12. This discredits the notion that the term "heaven and earth" refers to the cosmos because of the overriding concern before the Church was a covenant in transition.

Hebrews 8:13

13 In that he saith, A new covenant, he hath made the first old. Now that which decayeth and **waxeth old** is ready to vanish away.

The reference to the "foundation of the world" in the thirteenth chapter of Revelation cannot be viewed contemporaneously to the Mosaic covenant because the book of life and the plan for the Lamb slain for the sins of men preceded the event of Sinai for many generations.

Those who were in the book of life would include Abel, Noah, Abraham, and a multitude of faithful worshippers of the one true God. Therefore the transitioning of the covenants not only referred to the covenant codified on Mount Sinai but also referred to promises made to Adam that was passed down through the generational download until their fulfillment. Thus, the term "foundation of the world" in Revelation 13:8 identifies the entire covenantal ancestry of the book of life, including the ancient lineage that predated the Sinai.

8 And all that dwell upon the earth shall worship him (the beast), whose names are not written in the book of life of the Lamb slain from **the foundation of the world.** KJV

The Blood of Abel

The chronological placement of the expression, "foundation of the world," is further clarified in Luke 11:50-52. In a scathing rebuke to the Pharisees and lawyers, Jesus ascribed the cumulative liability to his generation for the slaying of righteous men from the time of _Abe_l to that of Zachariah. A curious notation to Abel weighs in dramatically with our contention that Hebrews 8:13 is a confirmation of the covenantal transition alluded to in Hebrews 1:10-12. This discredits the notion that the term "heaven and earth" refers to the cosmos because of the overriding issue before the Church was the transformation of the covenantal economy.

218

Luke 11:50-52

50 That the blood of all the prophets, which was shed from the *foundation (nt.2602)* of the world, may be required of this generation;

51 From *the blood of Abel* unto the blood of Zachariah, which perished between the altar and the temple: verily I say unto you, It shall be required of this generation.

For further study, it would be appropriate to examine the word 'foundation". The word foundation" highlighted through its Greek underpinnings shocks and amazed me with its clarification of the text at hand. The Greek dictionaries were unanimous in their definition of the word foundation as "katabole" *(n.t.2602).* The propagation of life was this word's proposed interpretation. Additional entries of "foundation" rendered "themelios" (2310). Further evidence that the translators of Western Bibles have failed to properly express the purpose of native Hebrew words even despite their greater influence over the translated text. The term "katabole'("conceiving seed") aids in clarifying some of the controversies of Covenantal Creation. The propagation of covenantal seed, or births if you will, is central in our contention that the theme of Genesis chapters 1-5 is of a covenantal nature. Thus, with such usage, the term "foundation of the world" essentially refers to the birth or conception of the covenantal world.

Foundation: NT:2602 katabole

lit., "a casting down," is used (a) of "conceiving seed," Hebrews 11:11; (b) of "a foundation," as that which is laid down, or in the sense of founding; metaphorically, of "the foundation of the world";

Foundation: NT:2602 katabolee, katabolees, hee

1. a throwing or laying down:
tou spermatos (namely, eis teen meetran), *the injection or depositing of the virile semen in the womb*, Lucian, amor. 19; Galen, aphorism. iv. sec. 1; used of *the seed* of animals and plants, Philo de opif. mund. sections 22, 45; spermata ta eis geen ee meetran kataballomena, Antoninus 4, 36; accordingly, many interpret the words Sarra dunamin eis kataboleen spermatos elabe in Hebrews 11:11, *she received power to conceive seed.*

Hebrews 11:11

11 Through faith also Sara herself received strength to *conceive seed*, and was delivered of a child when she was past age, because she judged him faithful who had promised. KJV

In Greek, there is an alternate sense for the word foundation that should enjoin our scrutiny. Its singular usage implies a structural (literal) or an initial lying down of ideas or principles (figurative). The broad usage of the English word "foundation" does a great disservice to the narratives in question. The nuances of properly evaluating this word will lead us to a greater understanding as to the original intent of the passages...

Foundation:

NT:2310 themelios

NT:2310 something put down, i.e. a substruction (of a building, etc.), (literally or figuratively):

The following text is a good example of the many times *themelios (N.T. 2310)* is translated in its properly defined sense.

2 Timothy 2:19

19 Nevertheless, the foundation (n.t. 2310) of God standeth sure, having this seal, The Lord knoweth them that are his. And, Let every one that nameth the name of Christ depart from iniquity. KJV

Hebrews chapter nine goes to great length by way of contrasting the bloody sacrificial system codified at Mount Sinai with the superior sacrifice of Jesus Christ. It is most important to realize that this former Sinaitic pattern of worship initiated in the time of Adam. The following text would not make much sense if it were strictly limited to Sinai because the intent of the crucifixion not only displaced the ceremonial law established at Sinai but also reversed the penalty for sin (death) decreed in Genesis chapter three. The statement accommodates both the foundation and the end of the old covenantal world, that is, the provisional atonement of animal sacrifice. The glaring suggestion of the finished work of Christ' on the cross— the putting away of
sin once and for all— is quite telling. The passage also helps in pairing the time of Christ's death and the end of the old covenantal age, or the end of the world.

Hebrews 9:26

26 For then must he often have suffered since **the foundation (nt.2602) of the world:** but _now_ once in **the end of the world** hath he appeared to put away sin by the sacrifice of himself. KJV

The chronological underpinning of Hebrews chapter nine reverberates in Hebrews chapter four. "The foundation of the world" of Hebrews 4:3 is strongly identified with "the seventh day" in verse four. The prophetic nature of Hebrews chapter four is a disclosure of divine intent concerning the "end game" for God's covenantal creation. The literary objective here was to illustrate for covenant believers that they had now entered into the seventh day, i.e., His rest. "The seventh day" points to Genesis Two as the foundation of the world in verse three. The apparent reasoning for this is to make a correlation between the prophecy of the first mention, i.e., the seventh day of Genesis Two and its fulfillment, as discussed in Hebrews chapter 4.

Hebrews 4:3

3 For we which have believed do enter into rest, as he said, As I have sworn in my wrath, if they shall enter into my rest: although **the works were finished from the foundation (N.T. 2602) of the world. KJV**
Hebrews 4:3-4
4 For he spake in a certain place of the _seventh day_ on this wise, And God did rest the seventh day from all his works.

Chapter 9
All Things

Modern universal doctrines would suddenly lose viability in the world of biblical exegesis if only the seven days of creation depicted in Genesis One were evaluated on the merits of their intended covenantal signification. Such universal assumptions are birthed within the skewed "cosmic" motif of Genesis One as perceived throughout Holy Writ, most notably in the writings of the New Testament. Understanding this aspect of Covenantal Creation is essential for correcting the misnomers applied by the broad brush of universalism. Its influence is perennial, pervasive, and its consequences have been devastating.

Genesis 1:3 spoke of the creation of light equated to the concept of the day. In most cases, references to the concepts of day and light in Biblical imagery have lent themselves to the association of some form of covenantal activity. The introduction of the first chapter of John focuses on the initiation of the ministry of John the Baptist; in essence, he was the forerunner of the light, Jesus Christ. The fundamental principle of the first mention is of utmost importance if we are to ascertain the imperative of placing the ministry of John as the initial phase for Israel's new covenant redemption through the preaching of repentance. John was, indeed, the forerunner of Christ's ministry. He was instrumental in bringing the nation of Israel to its knees.

The phrase "In the beginning…" (John 1:1) was undoubtedly penned to draw attention to its covenantal counterpart established in the first verse of the Bible. In effect, the first verse of the Bible functions as a summary of covenantal activity, and the second verse initiates its narrative. Why would the apostle John refer to a cosmic event in Genesis One to illustrate a point when his subject matter is wholly covenantal? The light discussed in the following passage refers to spiritual awareness and illumination as opposed to the notion of natural cosmic light. As noted earlier, John employed this expression and its related form to frame his narrative in a covenantal jargon. A discussion about the creation of natural light would have been perplexing, given the covenantal implications communicated by his writing.

The scripture, "All things were made by him; and without him was not anything made that was made," at first glance appears to support the prevailing view of a universal cosmology created by God. The expression, "all things," immediately evokes imagery of the creation account in Genesis One. Verse four then pursues a unique covenantal pattern with the introduction of light within the life of men. The division of light and darkness in verse five reacquaints us again with the same covenantal implications of Genesis One. The uncomprehending "darkness" of verse five is equated to the rejection of Christ by the Jews in verse 11.

John 1:1-5

1:1, In the beginning, was the Word, and the Word was with God, and the Word was God.

2 The same was in the beginning with God.

3 All things were made by him, and without him was not anything made that was made.

4 In him was life, and the life was the light of men.

5 And *the light shineth in darkness; and the darkness comprehended it not.*

11 He came unto his own, and his own received him not.

Verses nine and ten unveil the mystery of the text and its sacred purpose. If we were careless, the passage could lead one to believe that every person born into the human family possessed the "true light" of covenant illumination. Unfortunately, many have used this passage to support the view of universal salvation for all souls born into the human family. The usage of the word *world* in both verses nine and ten should not be viewed as cosmological but as covenantal. The text demonstrates that only covenant people are born into the true light of God's presence. Jesus focused his entire ministry to his people, the Jewish world, and they rejected his light. The Jewish world was founded through a covenant relationship and not through the creation of a universal cosmology. An important decision must be made by the student when evaluating the following passage: If the word *world* in verse 9 alludes to the covenantal world that produces a holy seed, we should also be consistent with the treatment of that word in verse 10. ...or will we revert back to a cosmological view of the word world when referring to the "world that was made by him?" How could that world (planet or solar system), inanimate objects, "know him not?" Verse 11 qualifies our covenantal assumptions by saying of verse 10 "He came unto his own, and his own received him not." ....

John 1:9-11

9 That was the true Light, *which lighteth* <u>*every man*</u> *that cometh into the world.*

10 He was in the world**,** *and the world was made by him, and the world knew him not.*

11 He came unto his own, and his own received him not. KJV (see also verse 5)

The exclusively covenantal application of the word <u>*world*</u> is employed many times in John's gospel. As we know, Jesus never traveled beyond the commonwealth of Israel during his earthly ministry. The following text duly draws the parameter of his comments by elaborating on the extent of his activities as confined to the covenantal world to which he ministered. We are not saying that every mention of the word "world" or "cosmos" applies exclusively to covenantal activities. As always, the text will determine its usage in each setting.

Most Bible students have assumed that Genesis One is a narrative of the creation of this cosmic world, or in many cases, the universe. Similar confusion exists with a sample of passages we have submitted below from the gospel of John. Both illustrations were intended to convey narratives regarding a covenantal world. Unfortunately, this misusage of the term "the world" has forged a universal motif unintended by the authors of holy writ.

"Rightly to interpret the Mosaic narrative, therefore, it is necessary to disabuse our minds of the assumption that it is a revelation of the primordial origin of the universe. How and when God originated matter and what were the first forms and modes of life-- whether of plants, insects, reptiles, fish, fowls, beasts, cattle, or angels-- It appears not the purpose of revelation to inform us; but this beginning of the Bible does inform us of the miraculous creation of man in the image of God." **Milton Terry. Biblical Hermeneutics. 1883. p.552**

The anticipated recipients of scripture were covenant people. Jesus came to the Judean world of his time, and those converted through the preaching of the Apostles. When we hear the words, "And God so loved the world…" we should once again ponder its implications as opposed to the implied universal position of cosmic reasoning.

John 18:20

20 Jesus answered him, *I spake openly to the world;* I ever taught in the synagogue, and in the temple, whither the Jews always resort; and in secret have I said nothing. KJV

A Universal World View

One of the greatest hindrances to deciphering the intent of scripture is the uncertainty of its scope and usage. Confusion usually has at its source the universal/cosmological view of Genesis One. When the terms "the world" or "all things" are cited, they usually evoke a scriptural range and purpose beyond Israel or the kingdom of God when, in reality, the objective of those terms was understood as local and covenantal. Although a creationist of sorts, but not of a modern ilk, Milton Terry understood that the configuration of the text did not permit a cosmological view to surpass precedence of what he perceived to be a local event. He did not understand the prophetic value of the text, but he surely understood its moorings to be embedded in a local environment…

"The first of Genesis describes a local and limited creation. How large a region it affected, and where that land was situated, are questions that now admit of no answer." **Biblical Hermeneutics. Milton Terry. 1883, p.551**

The covenantal view of Genesis One established its boundaries within the realm of prophecy with patterns intended for a particular grouping of people. The universal view that currently dominates Christendom also begins its journey in Genesis One. Its borderless declarations have inadvertently rendered a misappropriation of covenantal blessings and judgments unto a populace who never knew Him. It is of utmost importance that we examine this phenomenon because it is the root cause of the confusion the church is experiencing today as concerning "end-time judgment." Will God judge those who are alien to the realm of the covenant? By what standard will He judge them? Are they to be accountable for a gospel they never heard? These are some of the important questions that covenant creation responds to without the meanderings of denominational dogma that resists sound scripture and good common sense. We now consider several illustrations that show how the universal misappropriation of scripture has led the church into gross error.

God so loved the world

The scripture we will use as a prototype to illustrate our point will be John 3:16. The misinterpretation of the term *world* in John 3:16 is easily understood if we are consistent with its usage within the balance of the text. The first thing one must acknowledge is the historical setting in which the events of this passage transpired. The ministry of Christ was not to the Gentiles but the Jews. The focal point of that ministry was to rehabilitate God's people through a new covenant enacted through his death, burial, and resurrection. Verse 19 utilizes the word *world* in the same vein as John 1:10. Both cases allude to the covenantal world that rejected his message as documented in John 1:10 "He was in the world...and the world knew him not." Please note that verse 19 states that "light has come into the world" its roots are undeniably Genesis 1:3

John 3:16-19

16 For God so loved *the world* that he gave his only begotten Son, that whosoever believeth in him should not perish, but have everlasting life.

17 For God sent not his Son into the world to condemn *the world*; but that *the world* through him might be saved.

18 He that believeth on him is not condemned: but he that believeth not is condemned already, because he hath not believed in the name of the only begotten Son of God.

¹⁹ And this is the condemnation, that light is come into the world, and men loved darkness rather than light, because their deeds were evil. KJV

John 1:10-11

10 He was in *the world*, and *the world* was made by him, and *the world* knew him not.

11 *He came unto his own*, and his own received him not. KJV

The next scripture we refer to as the candy stick of evangelical futurists. Who would dispute the sentiment articulated in this passage? It plainly states that the Gospel must be preached to the *whole* world and *all* nations, and then the end shall come. According to futurists, the Gospel has not reached every domain on the planet; therefore, the end is yet to come. Although this passage appears to be a "got ya" moment, the unbiblical conclusions derived from this universal overreach fall flat on their assumptions as the word of God reproves such conclusions.

Matthew 24:14

14 And this gospel of the kingdom shall be preached in *all the world* for a witness unto all nations; and then shall the end come. KJV

If we are to remain consistent in our view of the covenantal world of the Gospel of John, the expressions *world* and the *whole world,* as referred to in Mathew 24:14, are essentially the same. It is the same world as "every nation out of Heaven" and the same world where "every eye saw him even those that pierced him." Copious scriptural evidence agrees with these conclusions. According to Colossians 1:21-23, the statements of Matthew 24:14, Romans 16:25-26, Romans 10:17-18 and Romans 1:8 agree with our findings that the Gospel reached the known covenantal world during Paul's ministry.

Colossians 1:21-23

21 And you, that were sometime alienated and enemies in *your* mind by wicked works, yet now hath he reconciled

22 In the body of his flesh through death, to present you holy and unblameable and unreproveable in his sight:

23 If ye continue in the faith grounded and settled, and *be* not moved away from *the hope of the gospel, which ye have heard, and which was preached to every creature which is under heaven;* whereof I Paul am made a minister; KJV

Romans 16:25-26

25 Now to him that is of power to stablish you according to my gospel, and the preaching of Jesus Christ, according to the revelation of the mystery, which was kept secret since the world began,

26 But now is made manifest, and by the scriptures of the prophets, according to the commandment of the everlasting God, *made known to all nations* for the obedience of faith KJV

Romans 10:17-18

17 So then faith *cometh* by hearing, and hearing by the word of God.

18 But I say, *Have they not heard? Yes verily, their sound went into all the earth, and their words unto the ends of the world*. KJV

Romans 1:8

8 First, I thank my God through Jesus Christ for you all, *that your faith is spoken of throughout the whole world.*

Regarding Mystery Babylon, the subsequent scripture enumerates the reasoning behind the judgments of a system that was responsible for the numerous martyrdoms of covenantal people. The usage of the word EARTH in the passage cannot be exploited with widespread implications because the victims of mystery Babylon lived in a well-defined portion of topography located generally in the Middle East.

Luke 11:50-51 delineates the historical timeline of its martyred victims from the time of Abel to Zechariah. This creates a chronological demarcation for the retribution of its victims. It does not provide the overreach of an international inquisition as those who posit such views.

.

Revelation 18:24

24 And in her was *found the blood of prophets, and of saints, and of all that were slain upon the earth*. KJV

Luke 11:50-51

50 That *the blood of all the prophets*, which was shed from the foundation of the world, may be required of *this generation;*

51 *From the blood of Abel unto the blood of Zacharias*, which perished between the altar and the temple: verily I say unto you, It shall be required of this generation. KJV

Our last statement may be very disturbing information for those who have assumed that Jesus died for the sins of all humankind. The scriptures have not implied such a sentiment, although its assumption is with us for many years. The scriptures plainly state that Jesus died for the sins of his people and for whomsoever he calls. Have you ever considered the scripture, "many are called, but few chosen?" If Christ died for every person born on the planet, the scripture would reveal that fact. The passage does not say or imply that **all men are called** *(an* unconscious assumption of our evangelical fervor). The word **many** denote a quantitative limitation. The word **few** heightens the qualifications of those appointed to the Gospel.

Mathew 22:14

14 For many are called, but few are chosen.

He Saved the Body

Ephesians 5:23-25 states that Jesus is the savior of "the body," meaning the Church. Verse 25 says that he loved the Church and gave himself for it. John 3:16 states that God so loved the world. There should not be any

233

difficulty in reconciling the two statements if we clearly understand the notion of what message was communicated by John in his Gospel when using the term *world*. The text is always the final arbiter in assigning the value of a word. A doctrinal orientation should never be allowed to modify the meaning of a passage. He saved his people from their sins (Matthew 1:21), but nowhere did the text implies Christ's sacrifice for the benefit of all humankind. The views that lend themselves to such conclusions disappear under the scrutiny of the overall text.

   Ephesians 5:23-25

23 For the husband is the head of the wife, even as Christ is the head of the church: and *he is the saviour of the body.*
24 Therefore as the church is subject unto Christ, so let the wives be to their own husbands in every thing.

25 Husbands, love your wives, even as Christ *also loved the church, and gave himself for it;KJV*

   The consistency with which the Bible refers to the redemption of the Church should aid us in reconciling the references to "saving the world" in John's gospel. The misapprehension of the Biblical expressions of *all things, the whole world, all* men and all flesh is understandable given the fact that we have been conditioned to perceive and misappropriate these terms in an all-embracing obligatory manner.

Acts 20:28

28 Take heed therefore unto yourselves, and to all the flock, over the which the Holy Ghost hath made you overseers, to *feed the church of God, which he hath purchased with his own blood. KJV*

1 John 4:14

14 And we have seen and do testify that the Father sent the Son *to be the Saviour of the world. KJV*

The following verses refer to the same subject, restating it in two ways. If Jesus reconciled the whole world (all of its inhabitants), then logically everyone is saved right now. It is not factious surmising on our part to disagree with this because many religious movements have utilized the apparent universal features of these texts to their confusion....

"In an interview with Robert Schuler Billy Graham said: *"I think that everybody that loves Christ or knows Christ, whether they are conscious of it or not, they are the members of the body of Christ.... and that is what God is doing today. He is calling a people out of the world for his name, whether they come from the Muslim world or the Buddhist world or the Christian world or non-believing world. They are members of the body of Christ because they have been called by God. They may not even know the name of Jesus, but they know in their hearts that they need something that they don't have and they turn to the only light that they have. And I think that they are saved and that they are going to be with us in heaven."*

2 Corinthians 5: 18-19

18 And all things are of God, who hath *reconciled **us** to himself* by Jesus Christ, and hath given to us the ministry of reconciliation; KJV

19 To wit, that God was in Christ, *reconciling **the world** unto himself,* not imputing their trespasses unto them; and hath committed unto us the word of reconciliation. KJV

Titus 2:13-14 and 1Timothy 4:10 are additional examples of a seemingly outright contradiction of terms, but they are reconciled through the statement, "especially of those that believe." They function as a kind of designated qualifier identifying the idiom and reference for the phrase, "all men"....

Titus 2:13-14

13 Looking for that blessed hope, and the glorious appearing of the great God and our Saviour Jesus Christ;

14 Who *gave himself for **us***, that he might redeem us from all iniquity, and purify unto himself a peculiar people, zealous of good works. KJV

1 Timothy 4:10

10 For therefore we both labour and suffer reproach, because we trust in the living God, who is *the Saviour of all men*, specially of those that believe. KJV

All Things

In the following passages, we will assess how the erroneous view of the term "all things" has led many to misguided notions that have perpetuated the universal creeds that abound in Christendom. The general implication of the phrase, "all things" is deciphered through the lens of our learned ecclesiastical assumptions. These cherished assumptions have led us to assume that these words interpret the scope of universal estimations. "All things" can mean whatever one wants to incorporate within similar statements. The Bible is unique in that its focus is purposely fashioned to conform within the context of covenantal means, goals, and events. It is most helpful for the Bible student to keep this important principle in mind when assessing similar terminology. Upon closer examination of the expression, "All things," something suddenly emerges that takes us off guard. 1 Peter 4:7 is such a passage. The proclamation that "The end of all things is near," should prompt one to inquire as to what things Peter intended to convey to his audience. "All things" could consist of any number of possible events or situations. When the time is taken to examine Peter's narrative, we discover his many references to the second coming of Christ; that is, the end of the Jewish age and its transition into the Christian age after the destruction of heaven and earth (Jerusalem and its Temple; 2 Peter 3:12-13). In other words, all events related to prophecies concerning the end of the old covenant "things" and their relationship to fulfillment in the New Testament. 1 Peter 4:7

7 But the _end of all things_ is at hand: be ye therefore sober, and watch unto prayer. KJV

Revelation 21:5

5 And he that sat upon the throne said, Behold, I make _all things new._ And he said unto me, Write: for these words are true and faithful. KJV

"All things" in scripture refer to covenant events, persons (men), promises, fulfillments, adversaries, dominions, etc. The expression does not refer to inanimate "things" within the realm of a three-dimensional sphere. This language does not permit a casual universal treatment in the New Testament. In Ephesians 3:9, Paul discusses the creation of covenantal things, not the things of cosmology. Once the conjecture of universal creation fades, the true objective of the passage will then accurately convey its message. The word "world" used in this passage is aion, or age and not earth. The questions remain 1. When did the beginning of the age begin?
2. Which age does this refer?

Ephesians 3:9

9 And to make all men see what is the fellowship of the mystery, which from _the beginning of the world (age)_ hath been hid in God, _who created all things_ by Jesus Christ: KJV

Revelation 4:11

11 Thou art worthy, O Lord, to receive glory and honour and power: for thou hast created _all things_, and for thy pleasure they are and were created.

Creatures and All Things

Hebrews 4:12-13

The narrative of the following passage is fairly straightforward. The symbolism utilized by the word sword effectively lends itself to the intended message; God is omnipresent, and there is no hidden agenda regarding his children. He knows all. In verse 13, he refers to the creature or creation as being naked before him. He says it another way, "all things are naked," or "neither is there any creature that is not manifest in his sight." Both expressions allude to the same notion that this scripture treats these words interchangeably in similar settings. The passage is illustrated in the ancient style of Hebrew parallelism as it reiterates the subject twice within the same verse; (although written in Greek, the author was obviously of Hebrew orientation). It is first rendered as "any creature" and then secondly as "all things." This is not to indicate that "any creature" is to be understood as all creatures. The "creatures" within the body of the text narrative (Hebrews 4:12-13) are covenantal creatures.

_12_ For the word of God *is* quick, and powerful, and sharper than any two-edged sword, piercing even to the

dividing asunder of soul and spirit, and of the joints and marrow, and *is* a discerner of the thoughts and intents of the heart.

_13_ Neither is there _any creature_ that is not manifest in his sight: but _all things_ *are* naked and opened unto the eyes of him with whom we have to do. KJV

Things in Subjection

What were "things" put under the authority of Jesus? The writer of Hebrews referred to those converted to Christianity. Those who were not as yet under covenant union were those who "now we see not all things put under him." (assurance of the future completion of covenant membership through the propagation of the Gospel in "bringing many sons unto glory.")

Hebrews 2:8,10

8 Thou hast put *all things in subjection* under his feet. For in that he put all in subjection under him, he left nothing that is not put under him. But *now we see not yet all things put under him.*

10 For it became him, for whom are all things , and by whom are all things , *in bringing many sons unto glory*, to make the captain of their salvation perfect through sufferings. KJV

Hebrews 1:2-3
2 Hath in these last days spoken unto us by his Son, whom he hath appointed heir of *all things*, by whom also he made the worlds (ages);
3 Who being the brightness of his glory, and the express image of his person, and upholding *all things* by the word of his power, when he had by himself purged our sins, sat down on the right hand of the Majesty on high;

Things are Given Life

The impracticality of the following statement should arrest inquiring minds as to its intent concerning the life-giving power imputed to the Church. When 1Timothy 6:13 says that God quickens *all things*, it can only refer to one theme. The propagation of life is fundamental to the work of God as life engages an eternal relationship with him.

1 Timothy 6:13

13 I give thee charge in the sight of God, who _quickeneth all things_ , and before Christ Jesus, who before Pontius Pilate witnessed a good confession;

Gathering all Things

The harvest of souls is another major theme that preoccupies the prophetic text. A notable example resides in the thirty-seventh chapter of Ezekiel, where God enquired of the prophet, 'Son of man can these bones live?" The gathering of God's people depicted by the breath of the creator and pointed to a Pentecostal rebirth in the generation of a new covenant.
Ephesians 1:10
10 That in the dispensation of the fulness of times he _might gather together in one all things in Christ,_ both which are in heaven, and which are on earth; even in him: KJV

The Creation of all Things

The New Testament creation motif inherited its underpinnings from the early pages of Genesis. Many scholars would disagree with such a statement, but the evidence is so abundantly contrary to this modern conventional position that several inquisitive minds have taken this group to task.

Ephesians 3:9

9 And to make all men see what is the fellowship of the mystery, which from the beginning of the world hath been hid in God, who *created all things by Jesus Christ* KJV

Colossians 1:15-20 is an excellent case in point. As the firstborn over all of cosmic creation, the passage loses credibility. If he is the first-born and Creator over the souls he reconciled unto himself, then we have a King of the highest order. Reconciling things in heaven and earth is why he came to earth. In understanding the concepts of heaven and earth, we understand why the "things in heaven and earth" desperately needed salvation. The old order of heaven and earth had to relinquish its standing to the new heaven and earth created by Jesus Christ through His death, burial, and resurrection.

Colossians 1:15-20

15 He is the image of the invisible God, the firstborn over *all creation*.
16 For by him *all things were created*: things in heaven and on earth, visible and invisible, whether thrones or

powers or rulers or authorities; *all things were created by him* and for him.

17 He is before all things, and in him all things hold together.

18 And he is the head of the body, the church;

19 For God was pleased to have all his fullness dwell in him,

20 and through him to reconcile to himself all things, whether things on earth or things in heaven, by making peace through his blood, shed on the cross. NIV

2 Corinthians 5:17-19

17 So if any one [be] in Christ, [there is] a new creation; *the old things have passed* away; behold *all things have become new:*

18 and all things [are] of the God who has **reconciled us** to himself by [Jesus] Christ, and given to us the ministry of that reconciliation:

19 how that God was in Christ, *reconciling the world to himself,* not reckoning to them their offences; and putting in us the word of that reconciliation. Darby

All Men/ All Flesh/Every Nation/All Tribes
Every Eye /Every Knee and Every Tongue

The crucifixion of Jesus Christ did not appropriate salvation for all of humanity as Dr. Billy Graham and the churchmen of his ilk have supposed. The grotesqueness of such a notion only debases the work of salvation to such levels of divergence that its consequence would be the total annihilation of Holy Writ. Inadvertently this results in an absolute denial of the true character of God.

The wheels of universalism have been slow at work, undermining the integrity and purpose of scripture, all the while contravening its power and vitality. The only reason Graham got away with spewing these views is that the church world today is Biblically illiterate. As similarly, the discovery of the Law in the time of Josiah; for years, they lived without its dictates and to their horror realized that they were living under a curse because they ignored the Word of the covenant.

John 12:32

32 And I, if I be lifted up from the earth, I will draw *all men* unto me. KJV

One of the greatest blunders of the universal cosmic motif is the view that all of humanity physically expires as a result of the Adamic curse. As we have discussed previously in this volume, spiritual death (the alienation from the presence of God) was passed down to the descendants of Adam. This view reinforces the concept

244

that the defiled covenant is conveyed through a particular lineage (Adam) and has nothing to do with the rest of the human family, the restoration of "life" for the covenantal family is to be spiritually born again as Jesus admonished Nicodemus in John 3. If the curse conveyed to Adam was a natural bodily death, then the reverse of that curse would amount to eternal physical life for all believers.

Romans 5:12 12

Wherefore, as by one man sin entered into the world, and death by sin; and so <u>death passed upon all men,</u> for that all have sinned. KJV

Can we "See" what God is saying?

When the word "see" is used in conjunction with a Biblical illustration, it usually denotes spiritual understanding and has little to do with the sensory perception of the eyes. For example, Jesus quoted the Old Testament scripture that "in seeing ye shall see and not understand" ....or in John 3, "ye shall not see the kingdom of God." Most Biblical students are aware of the apparent meaning of those passages, but when analysis for scriptures of similar value is challenged, attention magically shifts to the sensory capacity of human vision. It is amazing the involuntary responses the mind produces to avoid conflict with a particular theme that would potentially upset the denominational applecart.

Isaiah 40:3-5 and Revelation 1:7 are good examples of the situation at hand. On the one hand, we have a passage in Isaiah 40 that suggests that all flesh (every human) physically sees Jesus (the glory of God) during his earthly

ministry. Common sense informs us that it would be impossible for that to occur, but very seldom do we recognize that the Bible speaks to us in these ways. We often fail to spot these words, which function as a kind of marker as it designates the parameters of a discussion. If we allow the word _all_ to universalize the passage, we risk losing its proper historical context, and we end up offending its integrity by allowing absurd insinuations to be associated with the scripture.

Isaiah 40:3-5

3 The voice of him that crieth in the wilderness, Prepare ye the way of the Lord, make straight in the desert a highway for our God.

4 Every valley shall be exalted, and every mountain and hill shall be made low: and the crooked shall be made straight, and the rough places plain:

5 And the glory of the Lord shall be revealed, *and all flesh shall see it together*: for the mouth of the Lord hath spoken *it*. KJV

In the case of Revelation 1:7, we have an additional problem with the designating markers *all* and *every.* The illustration holds the greatest of consequences for those who have a vested interest in a futuristic bodily return of Christ and the destruction of the solar system as we know it. The historical value of how we view the markers (*all* and *every*) has profound implications for when Christ appears to judge his people. There are at least four very important issues at stake with the universal approach to this passage.
1. The historical context (when this happens?)
2. Audience relevance (who is the audience?)
3. How this appearance manifested?
4. Who will witness this event?

Every Eye Shall See Him

We cannot exhaustively assess the following verse because of its many important facets of prophetic detail; it would require a chapter of its own to access all of its riveting details. Our mission at this time is only to address the overreaching implications that modern Biblical interpreters have appended to this very important passage. The narrative they portray is one of a literal 5'7" Jesus returning to earth in literal clouds while every person on the earth views his arrival (even though half of the world would be asleep because it would be night time)! How this is accomplished remains a huge mystery. The traditional narrative in this passage falls short in so many ways. For example, the phrase, "They also who pierced Him," evidently places the prophecy of Revelation 1:7 in the first century, not in the 21st. The word "kindreds" denotes tribes, or more accurately, the tribes of Israel. The Jews pierced and crucified the Lord, not the entire population of the planet. All of this exposes Christianity to the scorn it so rightly deserves for promoting such an implausible story.

On the other hand, we may redeem our reputations by recognizing the prophetic and highly symbolic nature of the text by proceeding from that tenable standpoint. Yes, God can perform things beyond our imaginations, but we must not fail to remember one very important thing; He is bound to the prophetic patterns that he established in Holy Writ. Those who insist on violating those patterns create a transcendental new-age narrative that belongs to Hollywood and not from within the confines of the Bible. To be brief, we must strive for consistency in what we have discussed regarding the covenantal inferences of the word *all;* if we refuse, we abandon our Biblical moorings and left with fairytale-like narratives that are impossible to defend.

Revelation 1:7

7 Behold, he cometh with clouds; and *every* eye shall see him, and they *also* which pierced him: and **all** kindreds of the earth shall wail because of him. Even so, Amen. KJV

Every Nation under Heaven

Unfortunately, there are many portions of scripture whose details we overlook (even through a lifetime of study) that elude proper scrutiny indispensable to this discipline. Acts 2:4 neatly fits into that particular category. Rarely considered are the ramifications of the expression, "every nation under heaven?" I do not know of anyone who universalizes the verse because Acts 2:4 does not support such a notion. Upon closer scrutiny, verses nine and ten specifically delineate approximately 14 jurisdictions that are under the rule of the Roman Empire. The thrust of this passage is not preoccupied with Rome or its authority, but it is instead concerned with the rule, or the auspices of the kingdom of God in those provinces. Thus, the phrase "under heaven" denotes that these Jews are under its authority; that is, under heaven.

Acts 2:5

5 And there were dwelling at Jerusalem Jews, devout men, out of *every nation under heaven.* KJV

Young's Literal Translation correctly assesses the proper expression for the KJV's "creature" and inserted the correct word *creation*. The word creature has a wide implication in the world of Western thought, but its Biblical roots found in the world of the Hebraic idiom *bara*: to make fat, enrich, or to form. The proper correlations of the word *creation* in Genesis One must be held consistently if the Bible is to remain a cohesive text; otherwise, we are left with two distinct narratives concerning the subject of creation; one in the Old and another in the New Testament. Herein resides the mandate for modern creationism: the call for a reconciliation of these two divergent narratives for rehabilitation in a consistent hermeneutical narrative fit for the consumption of humankind.

Colossians 1:23

23 if also ye remain in the faith, being founded and settled, and not moved away from the hope of the good news, which ye heard, which was preached in _all the creation that [is] under the heaven_, of which I became — I Paul — a ministrant. YLT

All Flesh

"All flesh" is a familiar Hebraism denoting a great mass of mankind but not necessarily implying the absolute and universal totality of the human race. The common translation of the Hebrew word Eretz by our word earth is also misleading and the source of much false exegesis. This word denotes according to the common, usu loquendi, a limited territory, a region or a country and may always be properly rendered by our word land.
Unknown source

Isaiah 66:23-24
23 And it shall come to pass, *that* from one new moon to another, and from one Sabbath to another, shall _all flesh come to worship before me_, saith the Lord.

24 And they shall go forth, and look upon the carcases of the men that have transgressed against me: for their worm shall not die, neither shall their fire be

quenched; and they shall be an abhorring unto *all flesh.* KJV

Acts 2:16-17

16 But this is that which was spoken by the prophet Joel;

17 And it shall come to pass in the last days, saith God, *I will pour out of my Spirit upon all flesh:* and *your sons and your daughters shall prophesy, and your young men* shall see visions, and your old men shall dream dreams: KJV

Every Knee and Every Tongue

Romans 14:11-12

11 For it is written, *As* I live, saith the Lord, *every knee shall bow to me, and every tongue shall confess to God.*

12 So then **every one of us** shall give account of himself to God. KJV

When we were quite young in the Lord, we sang a chorus entitled, "Every knee shall bow and every tongue confess that Jesus Christ is Lord." The notion of Christians and unbelievers worshipping God in unison seemed to breach the integrity of what the Church is all about. The theme of separation from the ungodly regarding the covenantal relationship is foundational. The problem with my bewilderment stemmed from an implied concept that in the near future, God will reconcile all men through his blood. It troubled me for quite some time because the concept violated a great pattern of scripture concerning the exclusivity of our calling. But when I awoke to its true implications, I rejoiced in the Lord for his continuing revelation. The guiding maxim established by the Lord for this case is: some will gather, and the rest will scatter, many called, few chosen.

Matthew 7:13-14

13 Enter ye in at the strait gate: for wide is the gate, and broad is the way, that leadeth to destruction, and many there be which go in thereat:

14 Because strait is the gate, and narrow is the way, which leadeth unto life, and few there be that find it.

Chapter 10
The Breath of God

By studying the nuances of the Hebrew language, we have discovered some interesting hermeneutical patterns concerning the Spirit as "the breath of God." These patterns are regarding prophecy and about the covenantal creation of his people. The current perception of this subject has ensnared many into the practice of making glaringly errant interpretations of such passages. The consequences of this sort of philosophical speculation have produced a Western Gospel that, at best, only superficially mimics the intended Hebraic narrative.

The Hebraic culture and its language give us a fascinating view of the Bible's most profound implications. A discussion of its Ancient linguistic foundations should be considered. Hebrew words interrelated with what is called "parent," "child," and "adopted" root word associations give a strong indication concerning the fundamental nature or relationship one word has with other closely related words. This profoundly simplifies the study of scripture because these related words closely frame their intended objectives. Conversely, we oppose the practice of random selection of word lists, which very much resembles an arbitrary multiple-choice examination. Thus, root associations aid us in screening out the foreign influences that invariably create a distraction to the biblical narrative.

The recognition of this "root" association within a family of words essentially functions as an identifier for many Hebrew words. With this method of study, we essentially preoccupy ourselves with the investigation of the family tree of each expression to effectively prompt an intended montage as it yields its hidden treasures. The following scriptures indicate the Hebrew "root" associations in **Bold** to assist us in recognizing its location within a designated word. We will also include the Mechanical Version of Genesis to accompany these scriptures to bring a desired Hebraic dimension to our study.

Genesis 1:1

1 In the beginning God created the **heaven הַשָּׁמַיִם** and the earth. KJV

Genesis 1:1

in the summit Elohiym fattened the skies **(הַשָּׁמַיִם** and the land,   The Mechanical Version of Genesis (Benner)

The Hebraic rendering of the word "Heaven" essentially means skies or place of the winds. Its parent root is "sh-m" שם rendered "name". Notice these two letters (parent root) embedded within the word **sha-mayim** (skies or heaven הַשָּׁמַיִם. This will prove to be very significant as we wade a little deeper into the subject of the breath, name, and the Spirit of God about prophetic expressions in the Bible.

Ancient Hebrew words are written in consonants. Vowels assumed a local utility by those who read them. In Modern Hebrew, vowels are indicated by markings called vowel points to assist the pronunciation and uniformity for each word. Thus, creating a universal articulation of the language.

<u>Name:</u> **shem** (this is the parent root) שֵׁם

<u>Breath :</u> **neshamah** OT:5397

<u>Heaven:</u> **shamayim** OT 8064

This word also shares the same root, sh-m , as in the previous examples that we have noted. The language indicates that these words (heaven and breath) are also organically tied into the word "shem," or "name." In Hebrew prophecy, they both function synergistically. This will be of great value when we evaluate their shared functions in the realm of prophecy. The following Lexicons also allude to these mutual relationships

OT 8034 shem: Name: To mark with a sign to designate sign, stigma...to name
  Gesenius Hebrew Chaldee Lexicon to the Old Testament p.832

<u>OT:8034</u> <v@ **shem** (shame); a primitive word [perhaps rather from <u>OT:7760</u> through the idea of definite and conspicuous position; compare <u>OT:8064</u>]; an appellation, as a mark or memorial of individuality; by implication honor, authority, **character.**

(Biblesoft's New Exhaustive Strong's Numbers and Concordance with Expanded Greek-Hebrew Dictionary. Copyright © 1994, 2003, 2006 Biblesoft, Inc. and International Bible Translators, Inc.)

Shem: Breathe, breath. The wind or breath of someone or something is its character. Hebrew names are given to describe character. The breath of man is his character or what defines his being. The name of an individual is not strictly used as an identifier but expressive of his character and his breath. *Sky: place of the winds.* **Ancient Hebrew Lexicon of the Bible, Jeff Benner p.278**

English translations inadvertently obfuscate the important association that these root words have in common. What etymological relationship the English words "heaven," "breath," or "name" have in common in the Bibles that we have read? The answer is that there are absolutely no grammatical relationships in the English language that remotely indicates a compatible link to these three words. In Hebrew, the evidence to the greatest revelations is hidden in plain view beckoning for our perusal. We must investigate this linguistic pattern to clarify the muddled views of prophecy that are so rampant in the world of Christendom.

The first occurrence of the word breath in scripture is in Genesis 2:7. Its prophetic underpinnings about the covenantal birth are illustrated and maintained throughout scripture in very similar ways. Genesis 2:7 serves as an archetype for subsequent Biblical expressions that consistently relay the same narrative. For example (Ezek.37:9-14, Acts 1:2)

Genesis 2:7

7 And the Lord God formed man of the dust of the ground, and breathed into his nostrils the **breath** of life; and man became a living soul. KJV

7 And YHWH (he exists) of Elohim (powers) molded the human of powder from the ground and he exhaled in his nostrils *a breath of life* and the human existed for a being of life.

The English translation of the word *breath* cloaks the truth of very important teaching in holy writ. The Hebrew word rendered ne**sham**ah. Those who are vaguely familiar with Hebrew should recognize the parent root of that word as **shem** (Strong's 8034), meaning name. The Hebrews considered the word breath or ne**sham**ah (breath) to portray the character, status, or reputation of an individual. The bestowal of a name was usually due to an assessment of events related to a person's birth or a particular historical episode associated with their life. The name of geographical regions changed by a lost battle or a miraculous provision by the hand of God.

Genesis 26:22

22 And he removed from thence, and digged another well; and for that they strove not: and he called the *name* of it Rehoboth; and he said, For now the Lord hath made room for us, and we shall be fruitful in the land. KJV

Ruth 1:19-20

19 So they two went until they came to Bethlehem. And it came to pass, when they were come to Bethlehem, that all the city was moved about them, and they said, Is this Naomi?

20 And she said unto them, Call me not *Naomi*, call me *Mara*: for the Almighty hath dealt very bitterly with me. KJV

The conveyance of covenantal standing through the modification of a name documented in the account of Jacob thus engrafting the sons of Joseph into the commonwealth of Israel. In this case, the names Ephraim and Manasseh identified with the reputations of their forefathers, Abraham, Isaac, and Israel (Jacob).

Genesis 48:15-16

15 And he blessed Joseph, and said, God, before whom my fathers Abraham and Isaac did walk, the God which fed me all my life long unto this day,

16 The Angel which redeemed me from all evil, bless the lads; and *let my name(shem) be named on them, and the name of my fathers Abraham and Isaac*; and let them grow into a multitude in the midst of the earth. KJV

Covenantal adoption through the use of a name is a distinctive *modus operandi* of Yahweh in the gathering of His people. We believe that through the promotion of His Shem, the kingdom is defined. The progressive revelation of his character develops early in Genesis and elaborated within the balance of scripture. God's proclivity for mercy, deliverance, and wisdom was understood by Israel through His intervention into their most intimate affairs. References to the name of God in scripture are but a conflation of aspects and characteristics that serve to document that intervention. Thus, the orchestration of the development of the heavens and the earth was through the auspices of His Name.

Isaiah 62:1-2

For Zion's sake will I not hold my peace, and for Jerusalem's sake I will not rest, until the righteousness thereof go forth as brightness, and the salvation thereof as a lamp that burneth.

2 And the Gentiles shall see thy righteousness, and all kings thy glory: *and thou shalt be called by a new name, which the mouth of the Lord shall name.* KJV

His Name and the Church.

The Name of God and the Church allied in the most intimate terms through covenantal activity. All that is done for and through the kingdom is made possible by his name. The name and its impartation operate as an essential component of the new birth experience. The following passage refers to Christ's eradication of the Adamic curse. Conversely, salvation poetically depicted by the concrete imagery of the forehead, which associates the name of God with obedience to the human will.

Revelation 22:3-4

3 And there shall be no more curse: but the throne of God and of the Lamb shall be in it; and his servants shall serve him:

4 And they shall see his face, and his name shall be in their foreheads KJV

. In Hebrew thinking, there was little distinction between a person's name and formal public titles as we presently view them. The Ancient Hebrew viewed the name of a person to reflect his relationship to a family, tribe, religious, and social positions. In essence, no one activity or relationship truly defined as a person. These expressions functioned as a composite of an individual. Their name or reputation updated according to life's activities and achievements. For example, David was a king. When one referred to the king in David's time, both of the expressions "David" and "king" were understood to be the same person. He was also known as the Psalmist, the Son of Jesse, or "Ben" Jesse. The usage of the word David solely as an "identifier" was alien to the Hebrew way of thinking.

An excellent example of this principle is in Isaiah 9:6. According to our Western orientation, the scripture declares that the name (Shem) of that child is Wonderful, Counselor, Mighty God, Everlasting Father, and Prince of Peace. The passage does not assume that these designations were to be called titles, nor is there any inference to that effect. The scripture says his Name (Shem) shall be called.....

With this in mind, when we refer to the Father, we are essentially referring to Jesus because he is the subject of this prophetic picture. When we call on the God of Peace, we are referring to the same person. Note the usage of the word **His** in the singular. The scriptures never refer to God as "they," and therefore, the various functions or roles of the subject in this passage is Jesus. The word Jesus or Yeshua represents Gods' role as the Savior through the flesh of Christ. Therefore, we baptize candidates into the redemptive character" of God which is Jesus Christ. (Acts 2:38, 8:16, 10:48, 19:5) The following passage is written in Hebrew parallelism. This style of writing frames its subject through the repetition of its various aspects. We will attempt to illustrate our point through a careful recapitulation of the verse....

Isaiah 9:6-7

- For unto us a **child** is born
- unto us a **son** is given: and
- the government shall be upon **his shoulder**: and
- **his name** shall be called
- **Wonderful**
- **Counselor,**
- The **mighty God**
- The **everlasting Father**
- The **Prince of Peace**.

Do the Father and the son have a shared reputation or character?

Proverbs 30:4

4 Who hath ascended up into heaven, or descended? who hath gathered the wind in his fists? who hath bound the waters in a garment? who hath established all the ends of the earth? what *is* his name (shem), and what *is* his son's name (shem), if thou canst tell? KJV

Acts 4:12

12 Neither is there salvation in any other: for there is none other **name** under heaven given among men, whereby we must be saved. KJV

Acts 2:38

38 Then Peter said unto them, Repent, and be baptized every one of you in the **name** of Jesus Christ for the remission of sins, and ye shall receive the gift of the Holy Ghost. KJV

The name of God, therefore, expresses various aspects of his character, activity, and being. Thus, the references portraying God's provision, power, justice, and holiness viewed in scripture as his NAME or SHEM (character, breath, or reputation). Taking the name of the Lord in vain is equivalent to the misrepresentation of his character through a shoddy lifestyle of deceit or a lack of confidence in what he is reputed to be. For example, he is reputed to be holy. If we exhibit unholy patterns of behavior, we become guilty of taking the name of the Lord in vain. We truly become the people of his name when we identify and pattern our lives after the character and reputation of God. The New Testament approaches this issue most forthrightly in the following passages:

2 Timothy 2:19

19 Nevertheless, the foundation of God standeth sure, having this seal, The Lord knoweth them that are his. And, Let every one that *nameth* the name of Christ depart from iniquity. KJV

Romans 2:23-24

23 Thou that makest thy boast of the law, through breaking the law dishonourest thou God?

24 For the *name* of God is blasphemed among the Gentiles through you, as it is written KJV

The impartation of God's name (character) to his people is one of the primary themes concerning the covenant relationship. We are people of the "shem" or the name of God.
NAME :shem OT:8034, "name; reputation; memory; renown."
(from Vine's Expository Dictionary of Biblical Words, Copyright © 1985, Thomas Nelson Publishers.)

The covenantal implication of the term "breath" about God's identity sheds more light on the verse of Genesis 2:7. While we appraise the text in its covenantal light, "breath" in this passage assumes an additional feature as it imputes the name, nature, and character of God to his people. With this in mind, the "creation" of Adam may now be reassessed as we reconsider the allegorical, covenantal, and prophetic implications of the passage. Thus, "man" indeed became a "living creature" (or a living nephesh) in a covenantal relationship as also do those who continue to receive the spirit of adoption through the Holy Ghost today. Through this covenantal adoption, God confers his divine Shem, that is, his divine character or reputation to his children.

Scripture alludes to this as the image of God. When we are born again, we receive the ruash (Spirit). The prevailing notion that God made man in his "image" or that in some unspeakable way, Adam physically resembled God fails to fit the account as we have discovered.

.

Genesis 2:7

7 And Jehovah God formeth the man — dust from the ground, and **breatheth** into his nostrils breath of life, and the man becometh a living creature. (being of life) YLT
Genesis 2:7

and Yhwh the Elohiym molded the human of powder from the ground and he **exhaled** in his nostrils a breath of life and the human existed for a living being, **Mechanical Translation of the Bible (Benner)**

Additional textural evidence concerning the usage of the word neshamah (breath) in allusion to the reputation or character of an individual furnished in Job 27:2-4. The following passage aligns itself flawlessly with Genesis 2:7 as they are both employed in the same manner. They each divulge the covenantal nature and practical application of the Word in these related Biblical expressions. Verse three sets the stage for the divine character Job exudes in the fourth verse.

Job 27:2-4

2 As God liveth, who hath taken away my judgment; and the Almighty, who hath vexed my soul;
3 All the while *my breath (character) is in me, and the spirit of God is in my nostrils;*

4 My lips shall not speak wickedness, nor my tongue utter deceit. KJV

The breath of life illustrated in Genesis 2:7 serves as an archetype that initiates a pattern of covenantal birthings evidenced throughout the Bible. The imputation of God's character (His name) through the impartation of his Spirit began at the inauguration of the new covenant world and has continued into the present. The language and imagery remain consistently the same in the sample of scripture that we have provided within the balance of this article. The Old Testament entries are all rendered neshamah (breath). The New Testament entries are all variants of the same narrative with similar overtones.

Psalms 159:6 has always been problematic with its all-inclusive declaration of "ALL that breathe..." (or the KJV's "let everything that hath breath...) One cannot include ALL of humankind or all inanimate 'things". There has to be a logical realignment to the general text for this verse to properly adhere to the Biblical narrative. The accurate rendering of this word essentially possesses strictly covenantal overtones because only those who cleave to the name of God praise Him in truth.

If Psalms 150:6 reads in the purely Western manner that most adopt, the passage will lend itself to a universal interpretation inclusive of all human beings. *However,* not all who breathe with nostrils possess the breath or the ne**sha**mah of God.

Psalms 150:6

6 All that doth **breathe** doth praise Jah! Praise ye Jah! YLT

The Four winds

Heaven: the place of the winds

Ezekiel 37:9-10

9 Then said he unto me, Prophesy unto the wind, prophesy, son of man, and say to the wind, Thus saith the Lord God; *Come from the four winds, O breath, and breathe upon these slain, that they may live.*
10 So I prophesied as he commanded me, and the breath came into them, and they lived and stood up upon their feet, an exceeding great army. KJV

The insertion of the phrase "the four winds" in these two scriptures should not be marginalized. Both passages have to do with the gathering of God's elect and the rebirth of Israel. This imagery is nothing short of a recapitulation of the identical pattern of covenantal birthings found in Genesis 2:7. We must remember that a covenantal birth is no less a resurrection than one who was asleep for hundreds of years. The principle is the same: new life is imputed through the death, burial, and resurrection of Jesus Christ. The number "four" indicates from every quarter, or everywhere. The next passage describes the sounding of the trumpet indicating the resurrection of the dead that are gathered together from "the four winds immediately following the destruction of Jerusalem. This imagery is essentially an act of recreation established upon the foundation of Genesis 1:1 because it is here that God had prophetically created the heavens (the place of the winds) and the earth (not just a play on words). The act of creation, whether it is in Genesis or the book of Acts, requires uniformity of expression to function properly in the Biblical narrative.

Matthew 24:31

31 And he shall send his angels with a great sound of a trumpet, and *they shall gather together his elect from the four winds,* from one end of heaven to the other.

The words blow, wind, breath, air (109), and spirit are practically used interchangeably in the New Testament, especially when viewed in relationship with prophecy and its fulfillment. The covenantal implication of these terms fit neatly within the patterns established early on in Genesis.

Acts 2:1-2
2:1 And in the day of the Pentecost being fulfilled, they were all with one accord at the same place,

2 and there came suddenly out of the heaven a sound as of a bearing violent **breath**,(WIND KJV) and it filled all the house where they were sitting, YLT

WIND: NT:4157 pnoe (pno-ay'); from NT:4154; respiration, a breeze:

KJV - **breath, wind**.

(Biblesoft's New Exhaustive Strong's Numbers and Concordance with Expanded Greek-Hebrew
Dictionary. Copyright © 1994, 2003 Biblesoft, Inc. and International Bible Translators, Inc.)

BLOW:

4154 pneo (pneh'-o); a primary word; **to breathe hard**, i.e. breeze:

SPIRIT: NT:5594

psucho (psoo'-kho); a primary verb; **to breathe (voluntarily**

SPIRIT: NT:4151

pneuma (pnyoo'-mah); from NT:4154; a current of air, i.e. **breath** (blast) or a breeze; by analogy or figuratively, a spirit, i.e. (human) the rational soul, (by implication) vital principle, mental disposition, etc., or (superhuman) an angel, demon, or (divine) God, Christ's spirit, the Holy Spirit:

The commissioning of the Apostles recorded in Matthew 28:19, Mark 16:15-18, Luke 24:44-47 and John 20:21-22. In Luke, the verse reads, "he opened up their understanding to understand the scriptures"; in John it is recorded that "he breathed on them, and said receive ye the Holy Ghost"...

John 20:21-22

21 Then said Jesus to them again, Peace be unto you: as my Father hath sent me, even so send I you.

22 And when he had said this, *he breathed on them*, and saith unto them, Receive ye the Holy Ghost:
23 Whose soever sins ye remit, they are remitted unto them; and whose soever sins ye retain, they are retained KJV

Meeting the Lord in the Air

The last illustration that we will be submitting is one of the most controversial passages in the Bible. It is infamously utilized as proof positive for the viewpoint of the future rapture or catching away of the Church. Although this doctrine is new (1830), it does not deter those who promote its inaccuracies.

1 Thessalonians 4:17

17 Then we which are alive and remain shall be caught up together with them in the clouds, to meet the Lord in the air (109): and so shall we ever be with the Lord. KJV

Most of what is believed about this passage is contingent upon the interpretation of the word air (Strong's 109).They teach that the Church will receive glorified bodies to be Jettisoned through the atmosphere into the presence of God in heaven. Unfortunately, the imaginations of good people have been allowed to run amok without seriously considering the passage. The word air (Strong's 109) does not refer to the upper atmosphere at all; however, it does point to the lower atmosphere or that which we portray as nearer to our living space.

1. **aer** , Eng., "air," signifies "the atmosphere," certainly in five of the seven occurrences <u>Acts 22:23; 1 Cor 9:26; 14:9; Rev 9:2; 16:11</u>, and almost certainly in the other two, <u>Eph 2:2</u> and <u>1 Thess 4:17</u>.

(from Vine's Expository Dictionary of Biblical Words, Copyright © 1985, Thomas Nelson Publishers.)

There is another rendering for the English word air in the Greek that does fit the claim of a futurist reading (Strong's 3772), but it is not the one employed in this scripture. If Paul had used the word air (Strong's 3772), then the narrative of the rapture would perhaps have credibility, but he did not. Its proper usage illustrated in the following passage. The word <u>*air*</u> (Strong's 3772) used only eight times. Each entry has to do with birds or fowl flying in the atmosphere or sky.

Mark 4:32

32 But when it is sown, it groweth up, and becometh greater than all herbs, and shooteth out great branches; so that the fowls of ***the air*** may lodge under the shadow of it. KJV

<u>NT:3772</u> **ouranos** (oo-ran-os'); perhaps from the same as <u>NT:3735</u> (through the idea of elevation); the sky; by extension, heaven (as the abode of God);

(Biblesoft's New Exhaustive Strong's Numbers and Concordance with Expanded Greek-Hebrew Dictionary. Copyright © 1994, 2003, 2006 Biblesoft, Inc. and International Bible Translators, Inc.)

To Breathe

Let us now investigate the proper usage for the word air (Strongs 109). According to Strong's the word 'aer" means to breathe unconsciously or to respire (to blow air). This word has absolutely nothing to do with the atmosphere or the sky. Strong's links the words aemi (air) and psucho (to breathe). Nowhere do we find an allusion to the elevated sky or the upper atmosphere in these definitions.

AIR:

NT:109   **aer** (ah-ayr'); from **aemi (to breathe** unconsciously, i.e. respire; (inhale and exhale by analogy, to blow); "air" (as naturally circumambient): Compare NT:5594: **psucho** (psoo'-kho); a primary verb; **to breathe** (voluntarily but gently, thus differing on the one hand from NT:4154, which denotes properly a forcible respiration; and on the other from the base of NT:109, which refers properly to an inanimate breeze), i.e. (by implication of reduction of temperature by evaporation) to chill (figuratively):

(Biblesoft's New Exhaustive Strong's Numbers and Concordance with Expanded Greek-Hebrew Dictionary. Copyright © 1994, 2003, 2006 Biblesoft, Inc. and International Bible Translators, Inc.)

: **psucho:**

NT:5594 *to breathe, blow, cool by blowing*; passive, *to be made or to grow cool or cold*: tropically, of waning love, Matt 24:12.*

(from Thayer's Greek Lexicon, PC Study Bible formatted Electronic Database. Copyright © 2006 by Biblesoft, Inc. All rights reserved.)

1 Thessalonians 4:16-17 a prophecy was written in highly figurative language. The nature of prophetic

literature is to veil its mysteries through a parabolic/allegorical format. For instance, the prophetic use of the word *clouds* within this passage points to the gathering of the great cloud of witnesses both dead and alive under the auspices of His Shem or breath. 1 Thessalonians 4:16-17 expresses much more than a singular event in time, although it does point to its initiation. It perpetuates imagery of covenantal birthings that are well established in the biblical record and that extend throughout the ages. This imagery relates to the consummation of the age of Grace through the power of the Spirit in bringing fulfillment to the words of Christ in John 5. Christ appears to speak of two types of resurrection: one of a covenantal nature, through conversion, and another in referring to the resurrection of the dead. 1Thessalonians 4:16-17 refers to the amalgamation of the righteous dead and those who were alive and remained. The allusion to all having one breath points to the life-giving power of the Holy Ghost. The formation of the corporate "man," or Adam of Genesis 2:7, is a foreshadowing of 1Thessalonians 4:17 by way of representing the ideal of generation ingathering also depicted in the Sabbatical Feast of Tabernacles. (also called the feast of ingathering)....

John 5:24-25

24 Verily, verily, I say unto you, He that heareth my word, and believeth on him that sent me, hath everlasting life, and shall not come into condemnation; but is passed from death unto life.

25 Verily, verily, I say unto you, The hour is coming, and now is, when the dead shall hear the voice of the Son of God: and they that hear shall live...

28 Marvel not at this: for the hour is coming, in the which all that are in the graves shall hear his voice,

29 And shall come forth; they that have done good, unto the resurrection of life; and they that have done evil, unto the resurrection of damnation. KJV

The valid narrative of 1Thessalonians four does not introduce any similar incongruity which the modern teaching of the rapture promulgates. The rapture teaching appears as if out of nowhere as it manifests itself as an illegitimate child caught amid a hostile environment. The contention inspired by its intrusion into the Biblical discourse is legendary due to its patently absurd implications conjured without the sound balance of the chapter. In other words, the doctrine of the rapture disqualifies itself from being genuine dogma because it lacks the required relationship to an authentic Biblical pattern that would establish its pedigree. The definitions cited previously clearly state that the word air (Strong's 109) and its counterpart psucho (Strong's 5594) defined by the process of breathing. The imagery that this achieves in the text is its primary meaning: to breathe.

The task to sort out how this word operates in such a highly prophetic environment should be relatively easy. It certainly cannot mean the nonsensical, "We will meet him in the breath." This word picture correlates perfectly with the imagery generated by Genesis 2:7. When taking into consideration the centrality of God's name, its life-giving power, its identification to His character, we find agreement with an abundance of scripture that underscores the narrative of a "People of the Name." God achieves this through the gathering of His people under the auspices of His Name.

We must reconsider the established narrative of the text and the word picture that it generates. Its derivation is Genesis 2:7, where the breath of Yahweh animates the "living creature." The forming and breathing of this celebrated passage finds another Old Testament correlation in Ezek. 37, where the prophet is commanded to prophesy over the re-gathering of Israel through the Spirit of God.

Ezekiel 37:9-13

9 Then said he unto me, Prophesy unto the wind, prophesy, son of man, and say to the wind, Thus saith the Lord God; Come from the four winds, O breath, and breathe upon these slain, that they may live.

10 So I prophesied as he commanded me, and the breath came into them, and they lived, and stood up upon their feet, an exceeding great army.

11 Then he said unto me, Son of man, these bones are the whole house of Israel: behold, they say, Our bones are dried, and our hope is lost: we are cut off for our parts.

12 Therefore prophesy and say unto them, Thus saith the Lord God; Behold, O my people, I will open your graves, and cause you to come up out of your graves, and bring you into the land of Israel.

13 And ye shall know that I *am* the Lord, when I have opened your graves, O my people, and brought you up out of your graves, KJV

The accounts of a re-gathering of covenant believers via the new birth were alluded to by Christ and the Apostles. Biblically, the Name of Jesus Christ and all of its redemptive qualities utilized in every aspect of covenant life.

Colossians 3:17

17 And whatsoever ye do in word or deed, *do* all in the name of the Lord Jesus. KJV

In John 3..." Ye must be born again of the water and the Spirit," "Then Peter said unto them, Repent, and be baptized every one of you in the name of Jesus Christ for the remission of sins, and ye shall receive the gift of the Holy Ghost. Acts 2:38 KJV Thus, in prophetic imagery, the breath of God illustrates that all birthed into the family of God bear that Name. The gathering of His people in 1Thes.4:17 depict the Biblical objective of uniting and gathering the righteous dead with all those who waited for this appearing, or unveiling of the new kingdom.

Air; NT:109   aer (ah-ayr'); from aemi **(to breathe unconsciously,** i.e., respire; by analogy, **to blow); "air"** (as naturally circumambient): surrounding

KJV - air. Compare NT:5594. spirit (psucho)

In Addendum

Nostrils: The Gateway of the Spirit

When considering the imagery of the word *nostrils,* a few things must be taken into consideration regarding its metaphoric and covenantal implications, especially within the passage of Genesis 2:7. The function of the Hebrew word "aph" or nostrils seems to imply that it is the gateway of the Spirit to the unregenerated creature. The unconverted beast nature, with its will and passions, are thus subjugated and transformed through the shem or character of an individual imparted through the Spirit of God. We are not just speculating. The word aph reflects the emotional and spiritual propensity of a man. It is through the emotional profile that God converts his children.

. The lexicons cited below give an outline of this expression in scripture. The primary definition of the word means to breathe hard with anger or unbridled expressions of passion, including adultery and pride. Anger seems to be the primary usage of this term, but the overall usage of the word aph lends itself to a profile in man's emotional makeup.

The nostrils are also associated with the face or the forehead. The forehead evaluated as of the will of man. This is portrayed in the book of Revelation by the forehead as it signifies the submission of those who worship the Beast and the number which reveals his NAME.

Revelation 14:9

⁹ And the third angel followed them, saying with a loud voice, If any man worship the beast and his **image**, and receive *his* **mark** in his **forehead**, or in his hand, KJV

Revelation 15:2

And I saw as it were a sea of glass mingled with fire: and them that had gotten the victory over the beast, and over **his image**, and over his mark, *and* over the **number of his name**, stand on the sea of glass, having the harps of God. KJV

The English translation of the Greek word for the word *mark* is character. The theme of the previous scriptures is a portrayal of the character of the:
1. The Beast
2. God (respectively)

Just as the nature or image of God imparts submission through His NAME or shem, the antithesis of this is achieved through submission to the beastly unconverted nature in man. The word aph is also closely associated with the word countenance, face, or one's demeanor. The demeanor of a man is either subject to his beastly proclivity, or he consciously surrenders to the character of His Name.

Revelation 22:3-4

³ And there shall be no more curse: but the throne of God and of the Lamb shall be in it; and his

Servants shall **serve him**: 4 And they shall see his face; and **his name** *shall be* in their **foreheads**. KJV

OT:639 [a^ **'aph** (af) pa; from OT:599; properly, the nose or nostril; hence, the face, and occasionally a person; also (from the rapid breathing in **passion**) ire:

KJV - anger (-gry), + before, **countenance**, face, + forebearing, **forehead**, + [long-] suffering, nose, **nostril**, snout, X worthy, wrath.

(Biblesoft's New Exhaustive Strong's Numbers and Concordance with Expanded Greek-Hebrew Dictionary. Copyright © 1994, 2003, 2006 Biblesoft, Inc. and International Bible Translators, Inc.)

639 Aph Pa: Of frequent use in the phrase "to prostrate one self with the countenance to the ground." Gen.19:1; 42:6.

Gesenius Hebrew Chaldee Lexicon of the Old Testament p.69

Genesis 19:1

And there came two angels to Sodom at even; and Lot sat in the gate of Sodom: and Lot seeing *them*

rose up to meet them; and he bowed himself with his face (aph) toward the ground;

Genesis 42:6

6 And Joseph was the governor over the land, and he it was that sold to all the people of the land: and

Joseph's brethren came, and bowed down themselves before him with their faces (aph) to the earth. KJV aph is the root of the word utilized to illustrate the sin of adultery:

OT:5003 [a^n* **na'aph** (naw-af'); a primitive root; to commit adultery; figuratively, to apostatize

The relationship of aph to the expressions that we have cited also extends to the word bake. The apparent correlation of heated condition points to the underlying affinity that these words both share.

OT:644 hp*a* **'aphah** (aw-faw'); a primitive root; to cook, especially to bake:
KJV   -   bake   (-r,   [-meats]).

The emotional profile that we have briefly depicted is unique to the human condition. As a side note, we recently discovered that the word "man" in Paleo imagery essentially means "Whose hand works the fire."
        *Hebrew Word Pictures, Dr. Frank T. Seekins, 2012

The close relationship with the word fire in the Paleo is striking.
Fire: Man: yod   depicts a hand amid the fire. Thus, the ancient language continues to beckon us to evaluate the emotional nature of the man formed by God. The woman does not escape these corresponding relationships.

The word for woman is esha : "What comes out of man or what comes out of fire."

* Dr. Frank T. Seekins   *Hebrew Word Pictures, 2012

In summary, there are a trove of word relationships in the ancient Hebrew text overlooked by their prophetic associations. Those words are seemingly unrelated in Western languages, but they bear remarkable relationships when examined in Hebrew. When the words are placed in an established prophetic pattern, they function flawlessly into the intended Biblical narrative. In effect, this method of exegesis takes the study of scripture to a distinctively new level. It aids us by skillfully identifying a family of expressions rarely considered in the study of scripture. As the whisking of dust clears debris from the brush of a patient archeologist, so will the delusion of age-old fallacies vanish with the acknowledgment of original Biblical intent embedded within the ancient language of our faith.

Additional Works produced through New Jerusalem Publications obtained through Amazon::

- Elements Destroyed, Heaven and Earth Passing

- The Feasts of the Lord and their Fulfillment

- Appearing in Glory Aspects of the Resurrection in Covenant Creation

Made in the USA
Las Vegas, NV
15 June 2021